Lizzie McGlynn lives with her family in the Home Counties.

I Forgive You, Daddy

Lizzie McGlynn
With Jane Smith

headline
review

First published in 2009
by HEADLINE REVIEW
An imprint of HEADLINE PUBLISHING GROUP

2

Cataloguing in Publication Data is available from the British Library

ISBN 978 0 7553 1882 7

Typeset by Palimpsest Book Production Limited,
Grangemouth, Stirlingshire

Printed in Great Britain by
Clays Ltd, St Ives plc

HEADLINE PUBLISHING GROUP
An Hachette UK Company
338 Euston Road
London NW1 3BH

www.headline.co.uk
www.hachette.co.uk

Dedication

This book is dedicated to my brother Hugh and my Uncle Jim, who I still miss every single day and who I know I will eventually see again, and to my poor mother, who didn't have the strength to walk away from the man she feared so much.

What you are about to read is my account of my own childhood. I can only talk about what I saw and experienced for myself, anyone else's story is theirs alone to tell. This book is a work of fact. However, I've changed some of the names of people and places, as well as some physical descriptions, to protect the privacy of the individuals concerned.

Chapter One

'You've been a very naughty girl,' I said sternly, frowning and shaking my finger in front of my doll's face before suddenly clutching her tightly to my chest and whispering, 'But it's all right. I still love you. I won't let anyone hurt you.'

The light filtering through the windows made patterns on the carpet as I crouched on the floor at the back of my father's car, breathing in the rich smell of leather upholstery and feeling safe in the knowledge that I was out of sight of any casual passers-by. Then, rocking my doll gently in my arms, I began to sing her a lullaby, with my mouth pressed against her ear and my voice almost inaudible.

After a few minutes, I lifted her up on to the back of the car seat and steadied her for a moment before letting her slide gently down the soft, padded leather. Repeating the game over and over again, I became so engrossed in it that time seemed to stand still. And, for a few precious minutes, I could imagine that I was just like any other little girl, sitting playing with her doll without a care in the world.

Suddenly, there was a noise behind me and the door of the car flew open. Something struck me hard on the side of the head and, as I reeled from the force of the blow, my body slammed into the back of the front seat and I began to tremble uncontrollably.

'What the fuck are you doing?' my father bellowed, his voice cold with fury.

'I'm p . . . I'm p . . . I'm p . . . playing . . .' I stammered, trying to shield my head with my arms and turn so that my back would absorb the shock of the next punch.

'I'll give you "playing", lassie,' he shouted, grabbing me by the hair with one hand while the short, powerful fingers of the other closed tightly around my upper arm.

My father was a builder – a very successful one at that stage – and although he was quite small, he was strong, particularly when he was angry, which he seemed to be most of the time. My skinny little body was scrawny even for a four-year-old, and it must have seemed as light as a feather to him as he dragged me out of the car and threw me on to the pavement. Struggling to gain my footing, I could feel the rough ground grazing my legs, but it was mostly fear rather than pain that made me cry out as my father shoved me ahead of him through the front door and into the house.

'I'll – teach – you – to – get – into – my – car,' he raged, his words punctuated by punches and kicks that threatened to snap my bones clean in two.

I knew there was no point trying to explain. There was no point in trying to tell him that I hadn't meant any harm; that I'd just wanted somewhere quiet to play with my doll and had been attracted by the cocoon-like safety of the car. In fact, I knew that saying anything at all would simply enrage him further and prolong the attack, and that all I could do was take the blows and wait until my father either ran out of steam or lost interest in battering me.

As he flung me against the wall, and I fell in a heap on the floor, I suddenly realized that I was no longer holding my doll. I must have dropped her as my father yanked me out of the car, and the picture that came into my mind of her lying alone and abandoned on the pavement was for a moment even harder to bear than the pain and fear I was already feeling.

A familiar sense of guilt swept over me as I cowered in a corner of the hallway, my face pressed against the wall. But I knew that, however hard I prayed, no secret door was going to open up in the wall, and no gentle hand was going to reach out and pull me through it to safety. My father was in control, and there would be no escape from his brutal assault until *he* decided to stop.

He looked down with contempt at my limp little body curled up into a ball on the floor and snarled, 'Get to your room, and don't ever let me catch you touching my car again.' And then he turned on his heels and walked into the kitchen.

Sharp pains were shooting through every part of me as I crept silently along the hallway to the bedroom I shared with my older sister, Audrey, and sat, aching and exhausted, on the floor beside my bed.

The beating had left me in a daze, so I don't know how much time had passed before I heard my mother's voice shouting crossly, 'Lizzie! Do you hear me? Get yourself in here for your tea.' That evening, I waited even more impatiently than usual for my dad to go out to the pub. Finally, I heard the front door close behind him, and a few minutes later, I slipped out of the house to look for my doll.

Not daring even to touch the sides of the car in case my father was somehow able to see everything that happened anywhere in the town we lived in, I searched the gutters, the pavement and the bushes that ran along the edges of the gardens. But she was nowhere to be found. I imagined her having been picked up and chewed to pieces by a passing dog, or kicked down the street by some rough boy and then abandoned miles from her home, and hot tears of guilt and sadness streamed down my cheeks. I loved my doll; she was my only confidante and comforter. But, even more importantly, she was my responsibility, and I'd let her down. And now she was lost, and maybe lying alone and hurt somewhere, wondering why I didn't come and find her. Or maybe some nice girl had picked her up and taken her home with her, and she'd be somewhere warm and cosy with someone new to love her. It seemed the least likely of the possibilities, but it was the one I clung to as I crept miserably back into the house.

I was one of six children, born close together. In my earliest memories, we were happy some of the time, but any laughter in the house during the day stopped abruptly as soon as my dad walked through the door in the evenings. The whole atmosphere would change, and we'd melt silently into the background, trying not to give him an excuse to lay into us – not that he ever needed an excuse. His presence completely crushed my spirit, and I hardly dared to breathe whenever he was around, in case he noticed me and decided that something I was doing – or wasn't doing – deserved punishment.

However, ironically, in view of what was to come, Dad apparently saved my life one night when I was a tiny baby. He dreamed that a big hand was reaching down from the sky and choking me. It was such a vivid dream that it woke him up, and as he turned to look into the cot where I lay beside his bed, he saw that I was completely blue in the face. I was rushed to hospital and found to be very seriously ill with bronchial pneumonia, and I spent the next six months in an incubator. But maybe it was just a coincidence that he had that dream and then found me almost choking to death in my cot, and perhaps the hand he saw was actually his own, because for the next few years he seemed intent on trying to force the life out of me himself, in one way or another.

When I was a wee girl, we'd get a couple of presents at Christmas and a bit of pocket money now and again, and we'd club together to buy a bottle of fizzy pop and some sweets to share. Every week, Dad would give one of my older siblings some money and we would all go off to the cinema or the park, where we'd laugh and lark about with other kids. It wasn't until later that I discovered he was just getting us out of the way to leave him free to abuse Mum, who would always be sitting sobbing when we got home.

In the early days, we were just like normal kids whenever Dad wasn't there. When we were on school holidays, Mum would kick us all out in the morning whenever she could so that she could get on with the housework, and we used to scamper off together, happy to be set free. One of the places we often played was an old derelict house in our street, which was our make-believe home. No one ever knew we were there, and no one could get at us, so for a few hours we felt safe, although in reality we were probably in serious danger of plummeting to our deaths through rotten floorboards or of being flattened by chunks of falling masonry.

We used to call it the haunted house, because it was so old and creepy and just like the houses you see in old horror films. Its wooden doors would creak loudly as we pushed them open, and the wind blowing through the empty rooms made an eerie whistling noise that had the hairs on the back of your neck standing up. But we were never frightened there. We'd sneak in through one of the broken windows and play for hours. We even built a tree swing in the overgrown garden of the abandoned house, and used to have a fantastic time playing on it with other local kids.

It was one of the only times we ever really played with other children, because Dad wasn't there to see it and stop it. Perhaps more importantly though, playing in that house gave us a means of escaping from reality for a while. It was the nearest we ever got to being carefree kids, and the memories of the fun we had there are some of the few happy ones I have of my childhood. Playing in that house gave us the idea of making a den in our own back garden. Building it took us days, and we spent ages collecting bits of wood from all the empty, derelict houses in the neighbourhood, but finally we were able to stand back to admire what we'd built. We were really proud of that den, and played in it whenever we got the chance, until Dad wrecked it one day, in a typically violent drunken rage.

I went to ballet classes for a while when I was small, and absolutely loved them. My own parents would never have taken me, and my dad certainly wouldn't have paid for them. But my Uncle Tommy decided to take me with his own daughter, and to pay for my classes too. He was a lovely, kind man, and I couldn't believe how lucky I was. I often used to dream that I was grown up and dancing on a stage somewhere, and living a life like other people seemed to live.

But then, when I was six, my uncle's car went under an HGV in an accident; its roof was sliced clean off and he was decapitated. It was devastating, and a horrible image that I could never get out of my mind. And, of course, with my uncle gone, there were no more ballet classes for me.

His death reinforced a lesson I'd already learned very early on in my childhood – that almost everything in life is unpredictable. In fact, the only real certainty in my life was that rarely was a day going to pass peacefully.

My dad was always angry. He could be charming to people outside the family, but there seemed to be so much rage inside him that he wasn't able to contain it once the front door was closed. Even to this day, it makes me cringe when people praise him and say what a good man he was. He *was* a good guy, to his mates and to all the old-age pensioners who lived in the neighbourhood, and he'd often hand out vegetables he'd grown in the garden saying, 'There you go. There's a wee cabbage for you, and a turnip for your soup.' But behind closed doors he was a vicious tyrant who ruled his family with an iron fist, and there was simply no hiding from him.

He had a completely overpowering character, and he only had to be in the room, not even saying anything, to make me tremble with fear. I remember looking at him one day when I was older and wondering how he was able to induce such terror in me. He had wiry hair, an awesome temper and an extremely short fuse. However, his hold over me was mental as much as physical, and even the sound of his voice bellowing my name could make me sick with anxiety.

Living with my dad was like living in an army camp. We were all his personal little soldiers, and he used to bark out orders, like a sergeant major, and woe betide anyone who didn't carry them out to his own high standards. But I was only young, and although I really tried, I couldn't ever match up to what he expected of me, and the stress of trying to get things right – but not really understanding what 'right' was, and knowing that I wasn't going to manage it anyway – was incredible. My stomach was always tied in a tight, cramping knot, and my whole body seemed to be stretched taut as I waited, alert and anxious, for the next beating. And he didn't just use his hands. He'd use a leather belt, the hose off the twin-tub washing machine, even a chair. I was always covered in bruises in various stages of development – some dark, almost black, and others fading to a bilious yellow colour – and with red, painful, almost raw welts crisscrossing my backside.

Dad didn't need any reason to thrash us, but sometimes, particularly when he was drunk, he'd put something down and then couldn't find it again, for example, and he'd get into a rage and start shouting at us, accusing one of us of taking it. Then he'd line us all up in the hallway in order of oldest to youngest, and we'd stand there, shaking with fear, knowing what was coming and staring fixedly at the ground, trying to avoid catching his eye and enraging him further. He'd drag us out of line (although it was normally me who got into the most trouble) one at a time and start slapping us, shouting, 'Did *you* take it? Go on, own up, you fucking wee bastard.' Sometimes, someone would admit to whatever it was we were supposed to have done, just to save the others from a beating. But at other times, Dad continued to work his way systematically down the line as we stood waiting our turn, whimpering pathetically and begging him to stop.

On some days, the screams and sobs must have been loud enough for other people to hear them, but it was a different era then, and no one ever interfered. In those days, parents controlled their children in any way they wanted, and I suppose if people did hear anything, they just assumed we were getting the punishment we deserved, for whatever reason.

There was no bathroom in the flat we lived in when I was small, and I can remember being bathed in a metal bathtub that Mum used to put in the middle of the living-room floor and fill with water that she'd heat in the kitchen. We younger ones would climb in together, and Mum would wash us vigorously before lifting us out to be dried by Dad. It's the sort of memory that many people look back on with pleasure, but I dreaded bath days, because my dad would wrap me in a towel and fondle me, his face too close to mine and his rough hands grazing my soft, child's skin.

Dad had always made Mum sit in the front room while he thrashed whoever's turn it was that day in the hallway or a bedroom. But although I don't remember Mum ever holding or hugging us, showing us any sign of affection or giving us any sympathy when Dad beat us, she didn't actually hit us in those days, except for the occasional, almost automatic, cuff round the ear if we walked past her. At the same time, she rarely did anything to protect us from Dad. She was about an inch taller than he was, but she was just a wee timid mouse, and he used to slap her and throw her across the room on an almost daily basis. She was as petrified of him as we were. I've told myself for years that she had no idea what he was doing, and I still believe that, but it's sometimes a difficult belief to hold on to, particularly when you consider that he was doing it right in front of her eyes every time I had a bath.

Sometimes, when Dad had beaten me and I was lying, exhausted, on my bed, crying and in pain as I tried to ease myself into some position that took the pressure off the worst of my cuts and bruises, he'd come into the room and start running his hands over my pathetic little body, rubbing me in a strange, massaging sort of way. I hated the roughness of his hands as they touched my bruises, and I'd keep perfectly still, with my eyes shut, confused by the change from his apparently uncontrollable anger of just a few moments before. But, in contrast to his ferocious kicks and punches, it was almost like being caressed, and it was the nearest I ever came to feeling loved, which was what I longed for more than anything else.

Although Dad was always joking and laughing with his mates, his anger seemed to be constantly just below the surface, and it was as though beating me was his way of releasing the pressure. He never needed a reason; any excuse would do, and he thrashed me almost every single day, and often, it seemed, without provocation. He would pick me up roughly by the arm and hold me with one hand while he slapped me hard across the face with the other, letting go at just the right moment so that the force of his slap sent me flying across the room, my body, quite literally, bouncing off the wall on the other side. Then, by the time I'd landed like a bundle of rags on the floor, he'd be on top of me, kicking and punching me with all his might. I'd try to twist round and curl up into a ball, so that my back or my head was taking the worst of it, because bruises on my tummy always lasted a lot longer and were really sore. But often there wasn't time between the punches and kicks to get into a better position, and I'd just give up and let my body go limp.

Night after night, I'd lie in bed, muffling the sound of my sobs under the bedclothes and gently feeling all the lumps and welts that covered my body. I once heard Dad telling a friend of his that I was accident prone, laughing and raising his eyebrows about the scrapes I was always getting into. And whether his friend or anyone else believed him or not, it was enough to stop them asking any awkward questions. In fact, he had a ready-made excuse, because the railway line ran across the top of a slope at the end of our garden, and we were always up there playing. We'd stand beside the tracks as a train whooshed past, feeling as though the sheer force and speed would snatch the breath from our bodies and drag us on to the lines, and then we'd sit on the tracks for hours, just talking, until we could feel and hear the vibrations that signalled the approach of our next opportunity to dice with death. So Dad could laugh off all my injuries by saying, 'Kids, eh! It doesn't matter how many times the wee bastards fall down that hill, they just keep climbing back up it.'

And it was true that we probably did have more than our fair share of accidents, too.

Sudden, heart-stopping frights were a normal part of our lives, and we were in a constant state of nervous anticipation, waiting for the next one. But nothing could have prepared me for the ear-splitting sound of the gas explosion that occurred one day when one of my siblings tried to light the cooker with a clicker. With a feeling of absolute terror, I realized that the acrid smell of something burning was coming from my hair. My sisters and I all had hair long enough to sit on when we were children, and for a few moments it felt as though there was hot, molten lava sticking to my face and neck. I don't know whether the pain made me pass out, but the next thing I remember is someone wrapping a towel tightly round my head and then trying to beat out the flames that were lapping at the kitchen walls.

Dad would never allow us to go to hospital, even in situations of genuine emergency when he hadn't actually caused our injuries himself. So Mum cut away the almost orange-coloured remains of burnt hair from the side of my head and spread Acraflavin over my painfully singed flesh, and my burns were left to heal to scars without the benefit of any further medical attention.

On another day, I was playing on a big gate with a load of other kids, pretending it was a seesaw. All the kids on one side would jump at the same time and the kids on the other side would fall off. But I got out of sync, and my heels went underneath the gate just as everyone else jumped on it. The pain was excruciating; all the skin was ripped off my feet, which were flopping limply. I was helped home, but Dad just strapped my feet up with bandages and sat me in a chair, so the broken bones fused all wrong, and still stick out to this day.

However, there were a couple of occasions when my dad did take one or other of us to hospital. One time, when my younger brother Alex was little more than a toddler, he climbed up a door and fell off, straight on to the pointed end of the metal door handle, which snapped and stuck into his face. Dad had to be brought home from the pub, and he took Alex, who was screaming with pain and shock, to the hospital, where the doctors had to cut the door handle out of his head. The specialist told Dad, 'That boy is very lucky. That was within an eighth of an inch of his brain.'

My young brothers Hugh (nicknamed Shuggie since birth) and Alex were entrepreneurs, and they often used to go round collecting ginger-beer bottles to get money for sweets. One day, they asked some guy if he had any empty bottles, and he said, 'No,' but they could see crates of them behind him, so they went back later with my dad's wheelbarrow and helped themselves. After a few minutes, they shot out of there, Alex pushing the wheelbarrow and Shuggie on his bike, and as Alex ran across the road he called back over his shoulder to Shuggie, 'Don't go yet. There's a car coming.' The next thing he knew, there was a sickening thud and he turned just in time to see Hugh fly up into the air like a rag doll.

Convinced that Shuggie must be dead, Alex ran back to the house in a panic to tell Mum and Dad what had happened. But, by some miracle, Shuggie survived, although firemen had to come and untangle his bike from around his legs, and the story hit the headlines in the local paper – 'Rubber boy bounces back with only bruising'. And that was the one and only time I remember my parents being kind to any of us, because everyone knew what had happened and so they had to put on a show for the neighbours. Shuggie's legs were so badly bruised he couldn't walk for weeks afterwards and had to be carried everywhere. Dad bought him a remote-control car and sat him in the front garden, in full view of all the neighbours, so that they could see what good care Mum and Dad were taking of him.

One New Year's Eve, Dad was drinking in the living room with all his mates and I was sitting on the bed with Shuggie and Alex, telling them stories and making them laugh, when I heard Dad calling my name.

'Lizzie!' he shouted impatiently. 'Lizzie! Where the fuck is that girl?'

The boys' laughter stopped immediately, and I jumped off the bed, carefully avoiding catching their eyes. As I ran into the front room, the bitter stench of alcohol and cigarette smoke hit the back of my throat and I held my breath.

Looking at me suspiciously, Dad asked, 'What the fuck took you so long?' But, without waiting for an answer, he pushed a glass into my hand and said, 'Fill this up.'

Although I was only six years old, I was used to waiting on my parents and their friends, fetching and carrying their drinks when they were too drunk to stand up, and trying to clean up around them. So I turned and ran down the hallway and into the kitchen holding the empty glass. As a child, I never walked when I could run, and I was always darting from one place to another. It was partly my nature, and partly because anxiety was my default state; and it was as though I had a tightly wound coil inside me that made it impossible for me to move slowly.

I ran into the kitchen clutching my father's empty glass, and suddenly felt my feet slide out from underneath me as I slipped on a patch of spilled drink. I didn't even have time to reach out my free hand to try to break my fall before hitting the floor with a crash, my head smashing against the glass as I went down.

After lying there for a few seconds, with my cheek in a sticky, half-dried pool of booze, I tried to sit up. Then, still dazed, and with a sharp, piercing pain in my head, I became dimly aware of hands lifting me to my feet.

'There yer go, Lizzie,' a voice said jovially. 'That was quite a tumble you took there.'

Someone had pushed open the kitchen door, and I could hear another voice calling, 'Young Lizzie's had a bit of a fall.'

Holding on to the kitchen table to steady myself, I again smelled the familiar stench of cigarettes and whisky as my dad's face swam into view in front of me.

'Oh, she'll be fine,' he said. 'It's just a bump on the head. Get yourself off to your bed, Lizzie. And next time, be more careful. I've told you before about running everywhere. It's no more than you deserve for not doing as you're told.'

As I walked slowly and unsteadily down the hallway towards my bedroom, the pain grew worse. Touching my head cautiously, I could feel a large, damp patch of matted hair, and when I looked at my fingers, they were covered in dark, red, sticky blood. I felt a wave of weakness flood over me and I thought I was going to faint. But at that moment a hand caught me by the arm, and I heard the familiar voice of a neighbour who'd just popped in to wish everyone a Happy New Year.

'It's all right, Lizzie,' he said kindly, supporting me as my legs threatened to give way under me. 'I've got you.' Then, turning to look back towards the kitchen, he called, 'Someone get me a towel,' and a moment later he was wrapping something round my head to try to stem the flow of blood that seemed to be pouring out like water. But it was clear that he was having little effect.

'I think this wee lassie needs to go to the hospital,' he called again, this time through the open door of the front room, to my dad. 'That's a nasty gash she's got on her head there. I reckon it's going to need stitches. And she ought to be checked for concussion. Sorry to spoil the party, but this looks bad.'

The next thing I remember, I was in a car, and shortly afterwards I was lifted out and rushed into the A&E department of the local hospital. My dad was too drunk to hide his complete indifference, but the doctors and nurses were kind as they put stitches in the large, deep wound on the side of my head – which left another physical scar that's still visible today.

It's remarkable how resilient kids are, especially when they don't know that other children's lives are any different from their own – except, that is, that I had learned from a very early age that my father had complete control of my life, and I suppose it sort of followed in my young mind that all adults had to be obeyed.

I can remember being held in the arms of an older man one day while he traced his finger in a circle on my hand and played 'Round and Round the Garden'. But when it came to the 'tickly under there' bit, he didn't tickle me under the arm, like I always did when I played the game with my young brothers. Instead, he pushed his fingers between my legs and inside my pants. I was too young to know that what he was doing was wrong, but I didn't like it, and I began to try to wriggle out of his grasp. Then, looking instinctively towards my father to check that what I was doing was OK, I realized that the expression of disapproval on his face was aimed at me, and so I stopped trying to push the man's hand away and froze obediently in his arms.

There was one occasion not long after that when I was stopped by a man as I was on my way to the shops. Even when we were very young, my parents often used to send us to do errands for them, and this man spoke to me as I was running along with the coins my mum had given me clutched tightly in my hand.

'Well, hello there, lassie,' he said, smiling to reveal yellow teeth. 'You look like a bright wee girl. Do you happen to know where Hamish Brown lives?'

I pointed up the close towards Hamish's house, but the man didn't really seem to look in the direction I was pointing.

'No, I don't know which house you mean,' he said. 'Do you think you could show me?'

'But it's just up there,' I said, pointing again.

'Well, if you come on up there and show me, I'll give you 50p,' he answered.

Remarkably, despite all the experiences that had taught me that life was brutal, I was still a chatty, friendly little girl, always eager to please. So I led the way up the close. As I was bouncing along, gabbling away about God knows what, the man called on me to turn round, and as I did so I saw that he'd opened the zip on his trousers. I stood gawping at him in confusion for a moment, and he suddenly grabbed my hand and pushed it through the opening, saying, in a strange, hoarse voice, 'Just rub that.'

I tried to pull my hand away, but he held on to my wrist until I felt something wet spreading out over my fingers. The next minute, he was doing up his trousers, pushing a coin into my hand, and saying, 'I can find him myself. You can go on home now. Buy yourself some sweeties, and don't tell anyone.' And he turned on his heels and started to walk back in the direction we'd come from.

I knew something wasn't quite right, but I didn't understand what it was, so I didn't bother trying to tell anyone what had happened, especially because, whenever I did try to talk to any of the adults in my family, I was usually told to shut up. With colourful variations, 'shut up' was probably the instruction I received most often as I was growing up – in a life that was full of instructions.

Although being beaten regularly and having to live in constant fear of my dad was more than any child should have to put up with, as I say, I just accepted my life as normal. I wasn't really aware of what other children's lives were like, so I didn't have anything to compare mine with. But although, on the surface, I appeared to be a cheerful, feisty wee girl, I was very unhappy, and I tried to run away on at least a couple of occasions. The first time was when I was only six. I set off one day with a friend and just two biscuits, which we ate almost as soon as we'd left the house. We seemed to walk for miles, but I didn't even have any socks on, and it wasn't long before we were freezing and too tired and hungry to go any further. So we turned round and went home again, having actually only made it less than a mile up the road. Another time, I packed a bag for Hugh and Alex and took them with me, knowing that I couldn't leave them behind to face my dad day after day without me there to comfort and at least try to protect them. But we hadn't even reached the end of the street before we bumped into Dad, who turned us firmly round and marched us home.

By the time I was six, Dad was drinking heavily, and things began to unravel even more. Although I didn't understand what was going on at the time, I can remember several occasions when there'd be a knock at the front door and Dad would dart into the bedroom to hide before my mum went to answer it. I'd hear men's voices and then Mum sounding awkward and uncomfortable and making some excuse about Dad having been called out unexpectedly. It was the men who worked for him, coming for their wages, but Dad would have drunk all the money and couldn't pay them.

As his drinking got worse and his building business started to fail, he spent more and more time at the pub, and would come home late at night, drunk, and beat whoever crossed his path first when he walked through the front door. I already felt that it was my role in life to protect my two young brothers, and I lived in a perman- ent state of anxiety, listening for Dad's key in the lock and trying to hustle Hugh and Alex, and even Alex's dog, Fluffy, out of the way, even if it meant taking a beating on their behalf. I was just a tiny scrap of a child, terrified of my father, although still desperate for him to love me, but I somehow felt that I was more likely to survive his brutal attacks than my brothers, who I loved with a fierce passion, and who seemed to be even more vulnerable and fragile than I was.

Eventually, Mum and Dad lost their flat, we moved into a council flat and Mum started drinking heavily too. Things went from bad to much worse, and at the age of seven, my childhood came to an abrupt halt as I took on the roles of both wife and mother.

Chapter Two

Every weekend after we moved, the house was full of Dad's drinking buddies – after all, why pay pub prices when you can get a carry-out, do your drinking in the comfort of someone else's house and then fall asleep on the couch amid all the piss and vomit? Our house became the local hangout point for other heavy drinkers in the neighbourhood, and Dad was soon getting drunk every single day. Mum gradually joined him, and eventually most of the household's weekly income was being spent on alcohol. So, us kids had to learn pretty quickly how to look after ourselves.

Mum used to get clothes tokens for us from the social services, but she'd sell them to get money for alcohol, so our clothes were always tatty and full of holes. There was never enough to eat, and I was always hungry and would drink loads of water to make my tummy feel full. Mum and Dad would give us a few pounds on Saturdays and send us out to do the shopping. But what they gave us wasn't enough to buy food for two children, let alone six, so we used to steal things from the local shop, and change the price tags, so we would put tins of mince on the counter that apparently only cost 2p. The girls on the checkout must have known what we were up to, but they never said anything, perhaps because they realized we were waifs who'd probably starve to death if they didn't turn a blind eye.

We'd all go and do the shopping together – in fact, we seemed to have an unspoken understanding that we would try to stay together, to protect each other. We'd all learned at a very young age that we had to be vigilant, so we could pick up on what was going on around us. It got to the point where we could tell just from Dad's face which one of us was about to get it. All it took was a look; he didn't have to say a word for us to know what was coming, because we'd been conditioned by him for as long as any of us could remember. I was always on the alert, and if I saw him look at Alex or Shuggie like that, I'd quickly try to find some excuse to get them out of the house.

Some of the neighbours were really good to us and would give us hand-me-down clothes and bring round food, so we were lucky in that respect and some of them obviously had an idea of how bad things were for us. There were other people who were kind to us too; they probably didn't realize what a difference they were making to our lives.

Sometimes, after we'd done the shopping on a Saturday

and had been particularly successful at changing the price tags, we'd have a bit of money left over, so we'd go to the local baker's and ask for a bag of broken biscuits and buns. We'd hide them while we took the shopping home and sneak out later to eat them. I think the young helper at the bakery must have felt sorry for us, though, because instead of giving us all the broken, damaged biscuits that we asked for, she used to put all sorts of whole cream cakes and buns in a huge paper bag for us. We never dared look inside the bag while we were still in the shop, in case she'd put them in there by accident and suddenly realized what she'd done and asked for them back, but as soon as we were outside, we'd be pushing and shoving each other to try to get into the bag and breathe in that wonderful, fresh-baked smell. It still brings back the memory of those cakes whenever I pass a bakery today. After we'd hidden our treasure, we'd run home, drop all the shopping off and get out again as quickly as we could, our mouths already watering at the thought of the feast that lay waiting for us.

As my mum began to drink more heavily, she pretty much stopped doing any housework at all, and the flat became more and more dirty and squalid as each week passed. I hated the sticky mess that covered the floors, and the smell of stale cigarettes and booze that hit you as soon as you opened the front door. We were only children, but it was a constant battle trying to control the filth.

I used to sweep the floors, wash the dishes and help my sisters try to make something out of almost nothing for our dinner each night. Then, at the weekends, I'd mop up as much of the mess as I could and would use vinegar to try to wash off the greasy layer of tar and nicotine that covered all the windows and ornaments. That always left me reeking like a fish and chip shop. As time went on, some of my dad's friends used to stay over during the week as well as at the weekends, and it got harder and harder to hold back the tide of grime that threatened to engulf us all. I began to feel that we were fighting a losing battle.

I was always emptying ashtrays and picking up cigarette butts that had overflowed on to the floor, but however much I scrubbed and scrubbed at the carpet in the front room, it remained sticky with spilt drinks, which, for some reason, was one of the things I found most depressing to live with. Although almost no one except Dad's drinking mates ever came to the house, I still felt ashamed of the dirt that seemed to cling to everything despite all the cleaning I did. But perhaps an even greater motivation than shame was my determination that my young brothers were not going to grow up in squalor if there was anything I could do to prevent it. It seemed I'd become a house-wife before I'd even had a chance to grow up. I didn't want to be in the house cleaning and wondering what sort of drunken mood my dad would come home in. I felt as though I was being robbed of my childhood.

Social workers would turn up at the house from time to time, and I felt ashamed at the thought of them seeing the disgusting pigsty of a home we really lived in. But they only ever stayed for a few minutes, before making a hasty exit, somehow managing to ignore the fact that my parents were almost incoherent with drink and that we kids were having to try to cope on our own.

There was more than one occasion when I had to speak to a social worker through the letterbox. My heart thumping with fear in case my dad woke up, I'd put my mouth right up against it and whisper, 'I cannae get out. My dad's drunk and he's got the key under his pillow. I cannae open the door for you.'

I could just see this social worker's eyes as he bent down and peered through at me, and said, 'Well, come to the window then.'

'I cannae,' I hissed back, petrified in case the sound of my voice alerted my dad to what was going on.

'OK. I'll come back later when your dad's sober,' he answered, and then just walked away.

Amidst all the filth, we did have one luxury: a black-and-white TV. We loved watching the cartoons, particularly *Tom and Jerry*. But we quickly learned not to laugh out loud at them, because the sound of our laughter seemed to incense

Dad, and he'd suddenly come bursting through the door, grab one of us by the arm or the hair and give us a thrashing.

One day, Dad – apparently – had a stroke; although I think it was just a scam to get money off the social, because despite the fact that, after it, he used a Zimmer frame whenever he went outside, he seemed to be able to get around the house perfectly well without it. Some time afterwards, he was lying in bed one morning, sleeping off the alcohol from the night before, while Alex, Hugh and I watched cartoons, and before I could stop myself, I laughed out loud. The next thing I knew, he came flying through the door with the Zimmer frame raised high above his head and brought it crashing down on my skull. The force of the blow knocked me to the ground, and I felt a searing pain in the back of my head, as though my neck was being pushed down into my body. Completely stunned, I looked up from where I lay on the floor and was shocked to see a splatter of my blood across the walls and fireplace. But Dad just shouted, 'I'll fucking teach you to laugh at me,' and turned and walked out of the room.

A while later, my mum came in, and gasped at the sight of me. She was obviously frightened by the state I was in, and when she went out into the kitchen I could hear her saying to my dad, 'We need to get her to hospital.'

'She's not going anywhere,' Dad snapped back at her.

'She's fucking staying here. She's not opening her big mouth.'

Later, one of my sisters came in and said to Mum, 'You *must* get her to hospital. She could die.'

So my mum walked me up to my aunt's house – which was actually further away than the hospital – to get money for a taxi, and when my aunt examined the gash on my head, she turned deathly pale and sank down on to a chair, saying, 'Oh my God. I can see bone there!'

By the time we got to the hospital, my dad was already there, and he'd told the doctor some story about how I'd banged against a wall cabinet and an ornament on top of it had crashed down on to my head. I was given stitches (another scar), and my dad got away with almost killing me, again. And all because he heard me laughing at a cartoon and thought I was laughing at him.

Before Dad's business collapsed, we used to be given something at Christmas, but afterwards, what money there was went on booze. The Christmas I was seven years old, I'd told a social worker that I'd always wanted a dolls' house, and a few days before Christmas Day, when Mum and Dad were at the pub, I sneaked into their bedroom, opened their wardrobe door and found the most wonderful dolls' house imaginable.

I stood there for a moment, just staring at it, but I still

couldn't believe what I was seeing. Then, closing my eyes tightly, I prayed harder than I'd ever prayed for anything before, 'Please, God, please let it be for me. I'll be good for ever and ever. I promise.' Over the next few days, I sneaked into my parents' room whenever they were out and sat in the wardrobe playing with the dolls' house. It was as amazing as I'd always imagined it would be, and I'd be completely lost in another world, a world of toys and make-believe – a world that was actually home to lots of other children but seemed like a fantasy world to me.

By the time Christmas Eve arrived, I was so excited I could hardly get to sleep, and the next morning I jumped out of bed as soon as I woke up and went in search of the present that I still hardly dared believe was mine. I was given a few cheap bits and pieces, including a doll, which, any other Christmas, I'd have thought was a bonanza, but which this particular year I unwrapped almost with impatience, waiting for the one thing I really wanted.

Of course, I couldn't say anything about the dolls' house, because I didn't dare let my parents know I'd been sneaking around in their room. I kept hoping that they might be keeping it to give to me as a surprise if I was really good throughout the entire day. Although what made me think that there might be even the remotest possibility of my parents thinking up a way of giving me a nice surprise of any sort, I can't imagine. The day passed slowly. Mum and Dad kept drinking, and there were no more presents, and when I next got the chance to look in their wardrobe, it was empty. The dolls' house had gone.

A few days later, the social worker came to see us.

'Well, Lizzie,' he beamed, almost before he'd stepped over the threshold. 'So what did Father Christmas bring you this year?'

I bit my bottom lip to stop it quivering and answered him in as normal a voice as I could manage. 'I got a doll,' I said, swallowing hard and trying not to think about the beautiful dolls' house that some other little girl had been given. 'And I got a game, and I got a selection pack . . .' My voice faded away miserably.

'I see,' the social worker said briskly. Then, turning to Mum, he asked, 'Could I have a word with you?' and led the way into the kitchen, closing the door behind them.

I could hear Mum's muffled voice, and then the social worker saying angrily, 'Well, it was for Lizzie, as you very well know. I did not go to all that trouble so that you and your husband could sell the toys and spend the money on whisky. And what happened to all the other presents, may I ask?'

So the dolls' house *had* been intended for me after all. I couldn't believe how close I'd come to getting something I wanted. I tried to console myself with the thought that at least I'd found it and had been able to enjoy playing with it for a few days. It wasn't just the disappointment that upset me, though. I felt deeply hurt: it seemed as though everything good in the world was always going to pass me by. It looked as though I was never going to get anything I wanted, so there wasn't really any point in wanting anything. It was another harsh lesson learned.

After we moved to the council flat, Dad's beatings became even more vicious and his drinking got even worse. One night, something startled me awake, and as I lay in bed, confused and groggy with sleep, I realized that Dad was crawling up underneath my bedclothes. For a few seconds, I couldn't understand what was happening, but what my dad did to me that night was something so beyond the experience of any child that I could never have imagined it in my wildest dreams.

Ever since I could remember, he'd sometimes touched me in a way I didn't like, fondling and fingering me with his rough, bullying hands, and although I'd never understood what he was doing, I'd always had an uneasy feeling that it was somehow wrong. I'd soon learned, however, that squirming or trying to wriggle out of his grasp only made him press harder into the tender flesh of my body, and that it was better just to keep still and wait until he stopped.

My childhood had always been a nightmare, but what

my father did that night was to take away not only my virginity but, with it, my innocence and trust.

Later, as he left my room, he paused briefly in the doorway and snapped, 'Now, clean yourself up, and don't make me do that again,' and I felt that somehow whatever had happened had been my fault. Now I had another anxiety to deal with: as I didn't know what I'd done to cause or deserve this, how could I stop it happening again? Of course, it actually had nothing to do with anything I'd done – although it was many years before I realized that.

It was the beginning of a new nightmare, far worse than the one I'd been living until that day. After that night, whenever the house was empty, my father would drag me by the hair into the nearest room and hurt and abuse me in different and horrific ways. As he lay on top of me, filling my nostrils with the sour smell of alcohol and sweat, his unshaven face would scratch my delicate child's skin as he forced his tongue into my mouth, pushing it down into my throat and filling me with panic as I gagged and choked. It was horrible, horrible, and the memory of his abuse still fills me with dread and the same feeling of childish helplessness that I felt at the time.

After that first occasion, he began to develop a new pattern of attacks, often beating me and then forcing himself on me with loud, drunken grunts, enveloping me in a haze of booze and cigarette fumes and stale body odour, and then saying, 'If you ever tell anyone, I will murder your mum.' But sometimes he'd whisper, 'This is our secret. I'm teaching you to be loving,' and I'd feel a confusion of disgust and self-loathing, together with a flicker of hope that perhaps what he was doing to me was somehow a clumsy expression of some type of love. As I got older, the misery I experienced during his abusive attacks increased, because sometimes he'd do something to me that felt nice, and then I'd be overpowered by guilt. I didn't understand what he was doing, but I knew instinctively that it was wrong, and that by finding pleasure in it, however fleeting, I was doing wrong as well. He always seemed to be able to sense even the slightest response of my body, and he'd leer into my face saying, 'Does that feel nice? Oh, you liked that, didn't you?'

Alcohol and sex were the guiding features of my parents' lives during the years of our childhood, and there seemed to be no boundaries my father wouldn't cross. Despite her apparent indifference and her failure to protect us from my dad, I loved my mother dearly, which makes it even more painful to remember the images I have of her lying in a drunken stupor while some friend of my dad's had sex with her. She was too out of things to be aware of what was happening, and her sin was one of weakness rather than a deliberate, controlling evil, like my father's. It was impossible not to feel pity for her. But seeing her like that and hearing the horrible drunken laughs and grunts that came from her room simply added to the feelings of chaotic insecurity that were already so much a part of my life.

Then, one day, my dad came into my bedroom and said, 'There's somebody coming in to see you. Just you do what you're told.' A few minutes later a smartly dressed man in a suit was standing in the doorway of my room, smiling at me. I stood there, frozen in obedience and too frightened of catching it from my dad to do anything other than just accept whatever he did to me. And, after that, there were different men, all of them quite kind and well dressed. Dad would bring them into my room and say, 'This is my friend,' and then walk out and close the door. It wasn't full intercourse; they would just tell me to rub them, or they'd push my face into their penis and say things like, 'Oh, you're a pretty girl. Look at your beautiful blue eyes. Oh, you're being so good.'

Dad wasn't usually drunk when he brought his friends to my room, so he knew exactly what he was doing, and I assume their visits must have been pre-arranged. Perhaps he was getting favours from them in return. I hated doing it, and I felt hurt by it, but I knew it was just something I had to do, something people did to help their families. I knew deep down it wasn't supposed to happen, and we'd been taught from an early age not to speak about anything that went on in the house, so I never told anyone about it. I was always waiting for someone else to say, 'Oh, my dad brought his pal and I hated it.' But no one ever did. I just assumed that other people didn't talk about it because they didn't hate it like I did. And in some ways, it was better with my dad's friends than with my dad himself, because they weren't as rough with me as he was, and they were kinder to me. Sometimes, it felt almost like a loving thing with them, as though they were looking after me.

One day, my dad took me to a big building that looked and smelled like a school, and we sat on a bench in a hallway. My feet didn't reach the ground, and I sat swinging my legs and looking down proudly at the lovely clean white socks and shiny black shoes I was wearing. I felt pretty, all dressed up in clothes so unlike the threadbare hand-me-downs I was normally given to wear, and I was cheerful and happy.

After a while, we were taken into a large room, where some of my dad's friends were sitting around in chairs, and I was told to sit on one of the men's knees. I felt shy and embarrassed and pulled slightly away from him, and although my father's voice sounded firm but encouraging, the look he gave me told me quite clearly that I was to do as I was told. So I stood there obediently and allowed myself to be lifted on to the man's lap.

With his hand resting on my knee, he spoke to me

kindly, and I began to feel less frightened. Then he gradually started moving his hand up my leg and under my
skirt – and that's where the memory comes abruptly to
a halt. I can remember every detail of the building, what
I was wearing and how I was feeling up to that moment,
but, however hard I try, I can't remember what happened
next. I must have blocked it from my mind, although just
thinking about it still makes me break out into a cold
sweat and start to shiver uncontrollably.

I just accepted what was happening to me, until I was
eleven and we started having some basic sex education at
school. The other girls used to get together in huddles
and giggle as they told each other about their first kisses,
and although I was never included, I could hear what they
were saying, and it totally bemused me. They were talking
as though they'd never kissed anyone in that way before.
But that didn't make sense. Surely their dads must be
teaching them how to be loving, like mine was teaching
me? Me and my brothers and sisters weren't allowed to
go to anyone else's house, so I had no way of knowing
what went on in other families, and I certainly knew
nothing about boys my own age.

One day, a boy from school stopped me in the street
outside our house, and the next minute my dad came
flying out of the door in a rage. 'Get in the house, Lizzie,'
he barked, without looking at me. Then he turned to the

startled boy and shouted, 'And what the fuck do you think you're doing, laddie?' and proceeded to punch him, right there in the road in full daylight. Nobody intervened and, unsurprisingly, the local boys weren't too keen to stop and chat with me after that, and I wouldn't have dared to answer them even if they had.

Whenever Dad was in the house, I was always listening and watching. I tried never to make eye contact with him and draw attention to myself, but if I did ever catch his eye, he'd snarl, 'What are you fucking looking at?' and my heart would start to beat so fast that I'd think I was going to faint.

He'd often tell me to go into my room, saying, 'Get in and sit on that chair, and I'll be in to see you in a minute.' Sitting perched on the edge of the chair waiting for him was like a cruel torture, and I used to press my hands down hard on my knees to stop them trembling. I was so beyond any normal level of frightened that I'd sometimes feel a warm trickle of pee running on to the chair and down the backs of my legs. And then, when the door eventually opened, my dad would beat me for weeing myself – although, God knows, I was mortified enough not to need any punishment other than the shame I already felt.

Sometimes, I'd be playing outside when I'd hear Dad's voice calling me. My whole body would start to quiver and it would feel as though someone was standing on my chest, so that I couldn't breathe and fill my lungs with air. But I knew that I had to go in when he called me. And as soon as I took my first step through the front door, he'd take a swipe at me, slam the door shut behind me, and then grab me by the hair and start smashing my head against the walls. Then, after he'd finished dragging me up and down the hallway, cursing and swearing as he battered me from one end to the other, he'd send me to my room, and I'd sit on my bed, shaking with fear, knowing that the worst was still to come.

Eventually, my bedroom door would burst open and Dad would be standing there, already starting to unzip his trousers. He'd tell me to take my clothes off, and I'd have to lie naked on the bed while he looked at me and then touch him until he got an erection. He did it drunk or sober, and whenever there was no one else at home, it would go on for hours and hours, until I was in agony and barely able to walk. Then, when he'd finished, he'd often beat me again and tell me to keep my mouth shut or my mum would get hurt.

Every time my dad sexually assaulted me, I longed to curl up in a ball on my bed and be left alone. It's difficult to believe that no one had any idea what was happening, but if anyone ever did ask me if I was all right, I'd just brush them off with an answer that must have sounded sullen and bad tempered. On one occasion, when my mum went to see my aunt and left me at home with my dad, he started to abuse me almost as soon as the door had closed behind her. Later, when he'd finished and had warned me, as usual, not to tell anyone what *I* had made *him* do, he drove me down to meet my mum and dropped me off. I was tired and sore, and angry with my mum for leaving me alone with him, and when my aunt asked me what was wrong, I snapped back, 'Nothing.' Dad had taught me too well, and I was far too frightened of him and of what he would do to Mum even to dare think about telling anyone.

Day after day, I'd arrive home from school and tiptoe down the hallway towards my room, holding my breath and trying not to make any noise so I could spend a few minutes alone before starting my daily chores. But Dad had ears like a bat, and even when he was lying drunk on his bed, I'd suddenly hear his slurred, aggressive voice shouting, 'Who's that?'

There was no point trying to escape. My heart would thump painfully against my ribs as I pushed open the door of his room and stood there, with my head bowed and my eyes firmly fixed on the floor, while he cursed and snarled at me about some imagined wrongdoing. Then, a few moments later, I'd be bent over his bed while he brutally beat my backside until it bled and was so painful that I wouldn't be able to sit down properly for days.

On the rare occasions when I did manage to sneak into my room for five minutes before going to the kitchen to scrape together something for our dinner, Dad would appear at my bedroom door, bullying me and shouting instructions at me. Sometimes, though, we'd get home from school and Mum and Dad would be drinking and laughing with some of Dad's mates, and Alex, Shuggie and I would manage to make it to the bedroom unseen. We'd joke around together for a while and then start playing Monopoly. But it seemed that, however careful we were not to make any noise, the door would always burst open eventually and Dad would lash out and kick the Monopoly board into the air, sending all the pieces flying into the corners of the room, just for the meanness of it.

Quite apart from the evil, bullying, cruel side of my dad, he also had a childishly spiteful side, which was apparent in all sorts of ways.

My oldest sister was good at baking, and she'd sometimes bake treats for us, such as rice pudding and apple crumble, made with apples that Shuggie, Alex and I used to pinch from a neighbour's garden. One day, we were all in the kitchen, our mouths already watering in anticipation as we watched her make us a cake.

'It still doesn't taste right,' she said, dipping a spoon into the bowl and tasting the mixture. 'Here, you try it.'

She scraped the spoon around the edges of the bowl again and held it out towards us.

We loved it when she cooked for us, and we certainly weren't going to say anything that might annoy her and bring to an end this rare moment of enjoyment, but we had to agree that something wasn't quite right.

Suddenly, we heard a bark of laughter coming from Dad, who was in the living room. We all froze and looked nervously towards the door, but he didn't come in, and after straining to listen for a few more moments, we turned our minds back to the cake.

'Perhaps it'll be all right when it's cooked,' I said as I helped to spoon the mixture into a cake tin and put it in the oven.

While we waited for the cake to cook, we helped to wash the bowls and clear up the mess in the kitchen. Then, as soon as the cake was ready and it was cool enough to eat, we devoured huge warm, spicy chunks of it. It definitely tasted strange, but at least it filled a bit of the ever-present empty space in our bellies.

Later that same evening, Dad decided he was going to make us some tablet, which is a cross between toffee and fudge.

'Your sister can't cook,' he told us with a sneer. 'So I'm going to make something for you that'll be a *real* treat.'

We were amazed, but the tablet certainly tasted good.

It wasn't until some time later that we discovered he'd added Polyfilla to the flour our sister had used to make the cake, simply so that he could outshine her with his superior cooking skills. We were lucky it hadn't made us really ill – but that was the nasty sort of thing he did.

Everyone knew that Dad was trouble, and people kept out of our way to avoid getting dragged into it all.

One day when we were all at home, not long after I'd started at secondary school, there was a knock at the front door and, when my dad opened it, there was a man standing there with a big lad of about fifteen.

'Your daughter battered my son,' the man said angrily.

Dad just shrugged and called, 'Mary!' over his shoulder, and a few seconds later Mary appeared behind him at the door.

'No, it wasnae that one,' the boy said, shifting his feet uncomfortably.

'Audrey!' Dad called out again.

'No, it wasnae *that* one,' the boy said again, staring at his shoes.

'Elizabeth!' Dad shouted with a sigh.

'Aye, it was that one,' the boy muttered miserably.

Suddenly, his dad leant towards him and scalped him, shouting, 'Get yerself up the fucking road! Look at the size of her! *She* battered *you?*'

But to me it didn't matter what size they were. I'd take on anyone.

As Dad closed the front door, he looked at me almost approvingly and said, 'You get out there and give them a doing, Lizzie. If you come back in here beaten by anybody, I'm going to stiffen you. Don't you ever come in here and tell me anybody's beaten you. On you go. You're my wee champion. Yous'll make everybody afraid of this family.'

Dad was a horrible, evil man, who wouldn't give a second thought to putting a brick through the window of anyone who annoyed him. I can remember one occasion when he dangled some poor man out of the third-floor landing window, holding him by the ankles and shouting, 'If you *ever* try that again, I *will* drop you.' Dad was capable of aggression that was out of all proportion to his size, and he was the person his pals all turned to if they had any trouble of the smallest kind. For example, if someone parked in one of his mates' parking spaces, outside their houses or down the pub, they wouldn't talk to the person who'd taken the space about it; instead, a group of them, led by my dad, would go straight up to his house, smash in the door and tell him not to park there again.

Stealing was common in our neighbourhood, and when we were small we'd often be woken up in the middle of the night by my dad, lifted out of bed and taken to a factory or warehouse he was planning to break into.

Shivering with the cold, and still disorientated and groggy with sleep, I'd be pushed through an open window that was too small for any adult to squeeze through and told to go and open the door.

One night, Dad robbed the off-licence across the road and stole all the alcohol, cigarettes and money he could find. The next morning, he gave us kids some of the money he'd stolen and sent us over to buy cigarettes, and then watched from a safe distance. When we came out, he asked us what was going on in the shop and what the owner had said. Of course, we exaggerated all the bits we knew he wanted to hear, and then basked in the contentment of knowing that we'd made him roar with laughter.

Thieving was just a game to him, and he'd often show us his spoils and boast about what he'd got away with and how clever he'd been. And he conditioned us to follow in his fatherly footsteps. We grew up thinking that it was OK to take whatever you wanted without any regard for right and wrong. But there were always two cardinal rules: you didn't steal off your own, and you only robbed people who were more affluent than you were – which was almost everyone in our particular case.

Breaking into the sweet factory across the road was a regular pastime for all the local kids. We never got caught, because we'd been taught what to do, and we were never frightened, because we knew that it was what we were supposed to do. Afterwards, I'd show the sweets to Dad and he'd laugh and say, 'Well done! Give me some of them. I can flog 'em.' And I'd feel a warm sense of satisfaction that I'd finally done something right and earned his approval, despite the brutality of his behaviour towards me and his total inability to love or treat me with any humanity. However degrading and miserable my life was at his hands, however many of my bones he broke, and however many bruises, both external and internal, he inflicted on me, I still desperately wanted him to love me.

Chapter Three

The neighbourhood we grew up in was tough, and the kids at school were very abusive towards each other, but the regular, vicious beatings I suffered at the hands of my dad enabled me to hold my own with the worst of them. No one was going to hurt me more than he did. I hated seeing other kids being victimized, probably because I was so badly bullied by Dad, and I developed a reputation for stepping in to situations and sorting things out with my fists.

Back at primary school, I remember really enjoying library days, especially when 'the puffin man' came round selling Puffin books and we'd all sit huddled together on the carpet at the front of class while he told us bits of the stories to help us choose a book. I'd feel as though I'd been sucked right inside the story, and I looked forward to library days with a passion. They were a real escape from my childhood, which otherwise was one long, miserable endurance test.

Secondary school brought a whole new batch of anxieties. We were late almost every single morning, because

Mum and Dad would be sleeping off the previous night's drinking, so there was never anyone to wake us up. As soon as I got up, I'd rouse Alex and Shuggie, and we'd get dressed quickly and run all the way to school (although, in fact, Alex often slept with all his clothes on so that he could just step straight out of bed in the morning and be ready to leave). The blood would be pounding in my ears as we ran along the road, not having any idea what time it was but desperate not to be late for school. We were already objects of ridicule for so many reasons, I used to dread drawing even more attention to myself.

There was rarely any time to eat before we left the house – and usually nothing much in the way of food anyway – so it would seem a very long time till lunch. The worst mornings, though, were the ones when my parents *did* wake up, because then Dad would make porridge.

As soon as I woke up and heard him in the kitchen, it would feel as though something hard had lodged in my throat, and I'd have to keep trying to swallow to get rid of it. Then a griping pain would start in my stomach, my intestines would tie themselves in tight knots, and I'd start to sweat and shake. It was as if I was preparing myself to face torture, and the tension I felt on those mornings was almost unbearable, because, however hard I tried, I simply couldn't force myself to eat porridge.

I'd walk slowly and reluctantly into the kitchen, and Dad would thump a bowl down on the table in front of me and then stand over me, shouting and swearing, as my throat got narrower and narrower until it seemed to close completely. With my hair plastered to my face by tears, I'd be sobbing, 'I am trying, Dad. I am trying to eat it,' and sometimes I'd be sick into my breakfast bowl. But even that didn't stop him. Red in the face with fury, and with all the veins on his neck pulsating, he'd suddenly lose control completely and start shouting, 'You'll do as I fucking tell you to do, yer wee bastard. You *will* fucking eat it!' Then he'd push my face into the grey, congealed mixture of porridge and vomit.

Years later, I discovered that Dad used to take Alex and Shuggie aside on those miserable mornings and warn them that if they ever took any of my porridge, or did anything else to try to help me, he'd knock the fuck out of them. So they'd have to sit there, feeling desperately sorry for me, staring at the table to avoid catching my eye, as I tried to force cold lumps of the disgusting mess down my throat.

It wasn't defiance; you never tried to defy my father. It would never have crossed my mind to become involved in any kind of battle of wills with him, because there was no chance I could ever win. It was simply that I hated porridge, and once it also became linked to so many other fears and miseries, just the smell, or even the mention, of it could send me into a state of blind panic. Eventually I found a way round it, and as soon as I woke up in the morning and heard the sounds of my dad in the kitchen, I'd rush to the loo and fill the pockets of my school jacket with toilet paper before I sat down at the table. Then, when his back was turned, I'd spoon as much porridge as possible into my pockets and empty the whole disgusting mess down the toilet before I left for school.

Sitting down to eat a meal with my father was always a form of torture, and whenever we ate dinner together in the evenings, I'd pick silently at my food and keep my eyes glued to my plate so I didn't draw attention to myself. I'd long to escape from the table, and from the feeling of danger I always experienced when I was in his direct line of vision, but we were never allowed to leave the table until he'd finished his meal. He'd sit and stare at us coldly, slowly spreading butter on to a piece of bread while we kicked our legs under the table, desperate for him to finish eating and hoping that, when he did, we might be allowed to go out to play in the back garden until bedtime. Then he'd fire questions at us about what we'd been doing during the day. Once I was at school, he always insisted on knowing every tiny detail, from what I'd learned down to every single conversation I'd had and a description of every single person I'd spoken to.

The kids at school used to tease us because we always looked so scruffy and unkempt. The nylon socks I wore to school were hand-me-downs that were too small for me, and every time I tried to pull them up so that they'd look like the knee-high socks everyone else wore, I'd make another hole in the thin material. Eventually I decided to wear them rolled down as ankle socks. Sometimes a teacher would instruct me to pull them up in an effort to make me look smarter. My face would be crimson with embarrassment, and I'd be fighting back tears of shame, because I knew that if I did pull them up, everyone would laugh at all the holes. I can remember just one time in my entire childhood when I had a pair of cotton socks that I could pull up without making holes in them, and I was very proud of them, for as long as they lasted.

But although I couldn't do anything about the holes in my socks, or about the fact that all the clothes we wore were threadbare and several sizes too small, I was determined that they were going to be clean. Slipping further into alcoholism, Mum now did none of the clothes washing either, so I realized that if Shuggie, Alex and I were going to have clean clothes, it was going to be up to me to wash them myself, which I ended up doing almost every night. I'd rub and rub at the boys' socks in a bowl of cold water until my knuckles bled, trying, without success, to get them back to their original white colour beneath all the grey, ingrained dirt.

Although Mum used to wash the sheets from her and Dad's bed, she eventually stopped doing ours altogether. But nobody had taught us how to look after ourselves, or how to do housework properly, so I only ever washed our sheets when they were too dirty and smelly to sleep in, or when so much filth had transferred itself from the soles of our feet you could no longer tell what colour they were. Sometimes I'd try to make a game out of doing the laundry, and the boys and I would climb into the bath and jump up and down on the dirty bedclothes, chasing and bumping into each other as we bounced around the bathtub. It was fun, but the water was always cold, so our feet would be freezing, and we'd have to giggle almost silently so we didn't remind Dad of our existence and bring him, angry and swearing, to the door.

I was always trying to think up ways of making things fun for Alex and Shuggie and of giving them a few moments when they had something to laugh about. One thing I used to do when my parents were out was to march around their room waving Dad's walking stick in the air, imitate his voice and shout all the phrases he used, such as 'Always cover yer work,' and 'How's yer grannie?' Shuggie and Alex would laugh so much that tears would be streaming down their cheeks, and the thought that I'd cheered them up, if only for a few reckless minutes, would give me a boost for the rest of the day. There were many, many things that were needed in that sad little household, and laughter was high on the list.

After we'd done the washing, I used to wring out as much of the water from the clothes as I could and then hang everything around the bathroom to dry. But, however hard I tried, and although I used to put things under our mattresses when they were almost dry, to try to iron out the creases, us kids always stood out in our tattered, ill-fitting clothes, even amongst all the other scruffy kids at school.

To begin with, I was quite good at most of my lessons, although I'd find it very hard to concentrate, and the teachers were always telling me to pay attention. Sometimes, I was singled out in front of all the other kids in class for not having the right equipment, even though we'd go into shops whenever we could and steal pencils and rubbers and anything else we needed. Being told off for not having things made me feel very bitter, and I used to think, 'You try living in my house with my dad and see how important having a rubber becomes.'

So, it wasn't always the kids who were giving me a hard time. Looking back, I can't believe that no one I came into contact with picked up on any of the signs that something was seriously wrong at home. Although I used to fight back and pretend I didn't care, I hated always feeling like the poorest kid amongst all the other poor kids, and I often had to concentrate really hard to stop the tears spilling out when people sneered at me and called me names. Little by little, I retreated further and further into silence, showing everyone a cocky exterior when, under the surface, there was a turmoil of emotions and it always felt as though a loud, angry scream was rising up from deep inside me.

Even the kids who weren't openly hostile and aggressive towards me were often quite cruel, although I can't really blame them for that, because I must have looked like a wee toe-rag. My hair was always tangled and uncombed, my shoes didn't fit me, so my feet were all blistered and bleeding, and I was permanently covered in bruises. I came across as a really tough kid, and I can see why the teachers didn't like me either – although there were a couple of exceptions, such as a teacher I had in my first year of secondary school, who was an inspiration to me. She used to make a fuss of me because I was good at reading, and I felt as though she liked me, which was a feeling I'd never, ever experienced before. Being in her class was the only time I can remember having been happy at secondary school.

In the end, I couldn't bear the thought of going to school any more, and I used to wish I could just run and run, never stopping or looking back, and that I didn't have to try to fit in anywhere ever again. But there was nowhere else to escape to, no sanctuary to hide in for even a few minutes to get away from the taunts and bullying that were such a major part of every single day of my life. With no friends and no one to talk to and confide in, my young brothers became the centre of my world, even more than they had been before, and were the only things in it of any real value to me.

Not long after I'd started secondary school, one of the teachers took me into his room one morning and said, 'Well, Lizzie, the report that's come up from your primary school says you've got quite a reputation as a bully.' The expression on his face was serious, but his eyes looked amused.

'I only beat up anyone who hits my wee brothers,' I answered defensively.

'Oh, so what if I hit them?' he asked, laughing.

'I'd still go for you,' I snapped back.

'I can see I've got a character on my hands here,' he said with a smile. 'But you're going to have to stop. If you've got a problem with any of the other kids in the school, come to me, because this report follows you throughout your whole life, you know.'

I shrugged as I said, 'Well, I'm not going to be asking you for help!'

He leant towards me, suddenly looking more serious. 'What's happening here, Lizzie?' he asked. 'What's going on?'

He was a really good teacher, and I think he was offering me the chance to open up and talk about my problems. But what could he do to protect Shuggie and Alex? They were my responsibility, and I knew I couldn't trust anyone. Why would someone who was almost a total stranger be showing me care and attention when my own parents had never done so? So the fighting continued.

The reality was that I longed to be accepted, and every insult thrown at me by the other kids forced the pain deeper and deeper inside me and put another layer on the protective shell I was building around myself. I used to knock the living daylights out of anyone who was beating on someone else; I was doing what my dad was doing to me, but only ever to bullies. I wanted to hurt them, like I was being hurt, and to let them know how it felt. I couldn't hurt my dad, because he had complete control over us all, but I could hurt another bully at school and teach them the lesson I longed for someone to teach Dad. So I came across as a tough and rebellious kid, and it wasn't surprising that the other kids didn't like me. I did have one friend, though, called Jacky. I'd told her just a tiny part of what went on at home, so she always avoided coming into the house, but at least

I was able to spend time with her on the way to and from school.

I always dreaded going back to school after the Christmas holidays, because everyone would be talking about their presents. I remember once listening to all the other girls chattering excitedly and thinking how lucky they were when someone suddenly turned to me and asked, 'What did you get, Lizzie?'

I froze in horror, my mind racing as I tried to think what to say. Then, after a moment's pause, I said, 'Oh, I got a doll, and a selection pack,' and listed a few of the things that other girls had mentioned. In fact, the truth was that I hadn't received a single present that year, but I was too embarrassed and ashamed to admit it.

A few days later, there was a knock at our front door, and when I opened it, a couple of girls from school were standing there. I couldn't hide my surprise.

'Can we come in?' they said. 'We were on our way back from school and thought we'd come and see your presents.'

My heart started thumping. What was I going to do? Obviously they couldn't come in, because there was no way my dad would allow it and, in any case, I'd have hated them to see the squalor we lived in. But I couldn't explain all that. How was I going to put them off? And what was I going to say about my make-believe presents?

'I'm sorry,' I told them, fighting back the tears and trying to look as though I didn't care. 'I didn't get any presents. I was lying the other day. I didn't get anything for Christmas at all. And you'll need to go because . . .'

At that moment, my dad's voice shouted from the living room, 'Who the fuck's that?' The girls stepped back from the door with expressions of fear and disgust on their faces, and then turned silently on their heels and walked away.

I was devastated, and my cheeks were burning with shame. But then the thought struck me that perhaps they'd take pity on me. Perhaps they'd feel sorry for someone who'd had to lie because she hadn't had a single Christmas present and who was so obviously afraid to open her own front door.

No such luck. By the time I got to school the next day, they'd told everyone, and they were all laughing and pointing at me and saying, 'Ah, she's got to tell lies. She doesnae get anything for Christmas.' Not one person seemed to feel any sympathy or understand why I'd lied, and no one even thought to wonder why I hadn't had any presents. Ironically, I was the one who felt deeply ashamed.

I was always on the outside looking in at school, always excluded from everything that everyone else was doing – although one year I did get to go to a school disco. It was an evening at the end of my third year at secondary school, and, to my amazement, a girl I sometimes used to talk to came to the door and asked if I was allowed to go. I hadn't even bothered to ask my parents if I could, but one of my aunts was visiting that night with her girls, and she asked why I wasn't going. I made a lame excuse about not having the entry money or anything to wear – which were both true, as it happened, although not necessarily the real reasons why I hadn't even considered it.

My aunt shook her head and tutted at me, and then she and the girls took off some of their own clothes and dressed me up in them, and she gave me some money and sent me off to the disco. I felt both excited and anxious, as it was something I wouldn't normally have dared to do. But my aunt's support gave me the courage, and with my father at the pub, as long as I made sure I got home before he did, he'd be none the wiser.

I had the time of my life that night. At the end of the evening, I ran all the way home, and was in bed by the time I heard my father's key turn in the lock of the front door. I didn't fall asleep for a long time, because my mind was buzzing with excitement. It felt as though I'd been part of something that night, like a normal kid for a change.

Chapter Four

Alex had a dog called Fluffy when we were young. Dad used to kick the dog about and treat him as badly as he treated us, and he wasn't allowed in the house, although I often used to creep downstairs at night and sneak him into bed with me.

Sometimes, Dad would open the door of my room and stop in the doorway, sniffing the air, before bellowing, 'Is that fucking dog in here?' But that poor creature was dead clever, and as soon as he heard Dad's voice, he'd freeze and lie completely flat and motionless under the covers, so that you couldn't see even a trace of his outline, until Dad had left the room, and then he'd start shaking again.

He was a great dog. He was usually kept chained up in the garden, but whenever he was off the chain, he'd prance up the road to the school and sit outside the school gates, waiting for us. It felt like having a friend, finding him sitting there with his tail wagging and what looked like a smile spread all over his mongrel face. He used to disappear from the garden on his own secret errands, and we often wondered where he went. One day we decided to follow him as he trotted off up the road – straight to the back entrance of the local butcher's shop, where, after a few moments, someone came to the door and tossed him a few scraps.

I loved animals, and one day a couple of girls brought some tiny, bedraggled-looking kittens to the door.

'We found them under the floorboards of a derelict house up the close,' they told me, handing me one of the furry little balls. 'We're trying to find homes for them. Do you want one?'

I knew my dad would never let me keep a kitten, but even so I begged and pleaded with him, 'Please, please, please, Dad. Please can I have one?' To my amazement, he suddenly shrugged and said, 'Aye, OK.'

I thought I was going to burst with happiness, and for the next couple of days I didn't let that tiny kitten out of my sight. I played with it and cuddled it almost constantly, and poured into it all the protective love and affection that was bottled up inside me. Then, one morning, I heard a terrible noise coming from the garden and I ran out to see what had happened. Dad had let the kitten out and Fluffy had got hold of it. I knew it wasn't Fluffy's fault. It's a dog's natural instinct to chase a cat, and although he never tried to bite any of us, he'd been brought up to be nasty, so that was just the way he was.

I was almost hysterical with shock and distress, and

with anger at my dad for letting the kitten out when he must have known exactly what would happen. But I was also overwhelmed with a terrible feeling of hopeless guilt. I knew what my dad was like, and I should never have left the creature alone. It had been my responsibility.

Sobbing, I wrapped the kitten in a towel. Its little chest was barely moving, but there were wisps of air going in and out of its body, and as long as it wasn't dead, there might be some hope of saving it. So, clutching my pathetic bundle, I ran as fast as I could to find a vet. Knowing that my dad didn't just pick fights at home, but that he did it everywhere he went, especially when he'd had a drink, I decided to play it safe and, rather than going to the vet nearest us, to try to find one who didn't have any reason to dislike our family. I'd heard one of the girls at school talking about the time she'd taken her rabbit to a vet, and I thought I had a vague idea where it was, so I set off in what I hoped was the right direction. It felt as if I ran for ages, but finally I arrived and started banging on the door. After what seemed like an eternity, the vet opened it, and I thrust the kitten at him, begging, 'Please help me. My wee kitten's dying.'

'Oh dear,' he said, glancing at the bundle in my arms. 'I am afraid he doesn't look like he's going to make it, love. But let me take a look.'

He put the kitten on the ground and pulled back the

towel. After poking and prodding a bit, he looked up at me. He didn't beat around the bush. 'He's dead. Sorry, but it's too late.' He patted my head and went back inside, leaving me sitting on the doorstep holding my dead kitten. Dad let me dig a hole in the garden and, crying as though my heart would break, I buried it. But I couldn't get rid of the guilt and the knowledge that I'd allowed something so awful to happen to a helpless little creature I'd been responsible for.

Dad had tied Fluffy to a pole, and as soon as I'd finished patting down the earth over the tiny grave, he said, 'Fluffy's a bad, bad dog. Go on. Kick him. He killed your poor wee kitten. Beat him.'

As I approached him, Fluffy cowered away from me. I loved that dog and I never wanted him to be frightened of me, and I knew that what had happened wasn't his fault. But I knew also that Dad wouldn't stop until I'd done what he told me to do. So I gave Fluffy a couple of half-hearted slaps.

'That's no good!' Dad shouted. 'He's eaten your cat, for Christ's sake. He's a bad, evil dog. Hit him.'

Fluffy cringed and shrank away, looking up at me with fear in his big, sad eyes.

'I'm sorry, Fluffy,' I murmured to him. 'I know you didn't mean it. I don't want to hit you, boy. I'm sorry.' And I gave him another tap.

'Harder,' Dad shouted again from behind me. 'Go on. Kick him!' But, in the end, he lost interest, and I managed to get away with just giving poor Fluffy a couple of feeble smacks. Even so, he was never the same with me again, and I hated him looking at me with such fear in his eyes.

It was after the catastrophe with the kitten that Dad built us a pond and put some goldfish in it. It didn't go anywhere near making up for the loss of my kitten, but we still couldn't quite believe he'd done it. The next morning, though, he quite deliberately dipped some rotten, varnish-covered wood into the water, and not long afterwards all the fish were floating on the surface of the pond, belly up. I felt stupid to have been fooled into thinking that it was even possible that Dad would do something nice for us, and I knew that I should have been suspicious about it immediately. But children are so anxious to trust, and to believe that their parents love them, that it takes them a very long time finally to accept what would be glaringly obvious to anyone else. It was Dad's way of showing us that he was in control – he could give us things, but then he could take them away again – so it was never worth getting attached to anything, because the decision about whether it lived or died was entirely in his hands.

At one time, we had some baby rabbits. I used to love to cuddle them, burying my face in their soft fur, feeling the warmth of their bodies and the rapid beating of their tiny hearts. One day, I heard Dad calling me, and I ran into the kitchen, my heart thumping as I searched my mind to think of what I might have done wrong this time.

'Go into the garden and water my tomato plants,' he told me, handing me a jug. 'You can fill this from the water butt.'

Taking the jug he was holding out towards me, I ran out into the garden, opened the lid of the water butt and was starting to scoop out some water when I felt something bump against the side of the jug. Looking down, I almost passed out with shock. There, floating on the surface of the water, their sodden fur clinging to their pathetically dishevelled bodies, were my bunnies. I screamed and jumped away from the water butt, a wave of nausea washing over me as I turned back to look towards the house. And there was my dad, standing at the kitchen window, watching me and laughing with delight.

He may have felt a cruel satisfaction at the sight of the tears that were flooding down my cheeks, but he would have been shocked if he'd been able to see the anger and hatred for him that filled my heart at that moment. He was a monster who loved nothing better than hurting anyone or anything that was weaker than he was, and he took great pleasure in destroying everything I loved. It became a point of honour for me not to show how much he was hurting me, and that day I battled to swallow the fury and resentment I felt towards him.

I remember our one and only family holiday, staying in a flat by the coast that belonged to a friend of my dad's. Us kids spent a week alone with Mum, and Dad joined us for a second week. Being there without him was fantastic. We didn't have to watch for him coming home every day, and we could laugh and run around together like normal kids. I can remember standing on the quay on the day he was due to arrive, watching the ferry as it sailed closer and closer and almost willing something to happen to it so that he'd never reach us on the shore. I imagined it disappearing suddenly beneath the waves while we all waited for it to pop up again when the swell subsided. And then all the fuss there'd be when it didn't appear, and how I'd be secretly thanking God for the fact that I wouldn't ever have to put up with the horrible, unremitting sexual and physical abuse that was the only thing my dad's presence meant to me.

I'd called out and prevented him accidentally poisoning himself one night when he was in the greenhouse at home and too drunk to realize that he was about to take a swig from a bottle of Paraquat. I often wondered afterwards why I hadn't just let him drink it – at least it would have put an end to all my suffering – although I knew I simply couldn't have lived with myself if I had. But if the ferry he was on were to sink, that would be completely different, because it wouldn't be anything that I had any control over. Even so, I still felt guilty for thinking about it.

So I stood on the quay that day, watching the boat grow bigger and bigger, with fear and dread building up inside me until I thought I'd burst and, eventually, the ferry docked and my father was standing in front of me again.

Later that day, we played on the swings in a park near the flat. I had decided to wear my swimming costume underneath my clothes and was just about to strip off and go for a swim when I noticed my father crouched down amongst the bushes beside the playground. My skin started to crawl and I became convinced he was spying on me. His eyes were firmly fixed on me, and I quickly abandoned my plan to play in the sea. A shudder ran through me as I edged closer to my siblings, hoping for safety in numbers.

The first night after Dad arrived, he took Mum out to the pub, and I lay wide awake in bed, too anxious to close my eyes and try to sleep until I heard them come back and stumble up the stairs. Mum was so drunk that she immediately collapsed into bed and began snoring loudly, but I couldn't hear any sounds that indicated Dad had done the same. Sure enough, a few seconds later, even with my eyes tightly shut, I could sense that he was standing in the doorway of my room.

I kept completely still, listening to him blundering about

in the dark of the bedroom and then smelled the sour, stale smell of his breath enveloping me as he leant down towards me and hissed in a loud whisper, his voice thick with drink, 'Elizabeth! Lizzie! Get up and come with me.'

For what seemed like an eternity, I lay rigid with fear beside my almost comatose mother as my father touched my body and then pushed his finger inside me before taking my hand and guiding it firmly towards his penis. I tried to block out what was happening and to turn my head away from the foul stench of his body, but I couldn't stop the thought that kept going round and round in my head: why wasn't someone coming to help me?

That week seemed to drag on even more slowly and miserably than a week at home. Almost every day, Dad made us wade out, stand in the freezing seawater until our legs and feet were stinging with the cold, and collect mussels and clams, prising them off the rocks until our hands were so numb they ached and the blood froze in our veins before it reached the cut surfaces of our fingers. Then, when he finally thought we'd collected enough, he sold them to the local fishmonger to help fund the night's boozing. He'd often insist that we stayed in the icy black water until it was so dark we could barely see the shore, and when we begged to be allowed to stop, he just laughed, and promised that, if we collected one more batch, he'd cook some for us when we got back to the flat, which he actually did do, once.

During the day, he'd stand at a window in the flat and toss some of the clams we'd collected to the seagulls that circled noisily overhead. But he had soaked the clams in bleach, and the seagulls would dive and catch them in mid-air and then make a horrible, strangled, screeching sound, which would stop abruptly as they hit the ground. Dad would laugh with delighted amusement, but I'd put my hands over my ears to try to block out the hideous noise. I hated to see the birds suffer, and I thought I knew just how they felt – their excited anticipation as they saw the delicious food, and then the shock and pain as they realized, too late, that what they'd thought was a treat was actually something dangerous and harmful. And I felt, again, that familiar feeling of guilt which followed me throughout my childhood, because the seagulls were being killed by clams that *I* had gathered.

There were some other kids where we were staying, but they obviously sensed our vulnerability and 'otherness' immediately, and made up a song about us, which they sang to the tune of the Addams Family song:

> Their hoos is awful smelly
> They feed off bread and jelly
> They can't afford a telly
> The eejiot family.

We knew we were scruffy – it was a fact we couldn't hide or change. So we were cheeky and defiant in return. But their taunts were really hurtful, and when no one was looking, Alex, Shuggie and I would sit and have a cuddle and cry, and I'd tell them, 'Everything's going to be OK one day,' although I don't think they believed that any more than I did.

Chapter Five

'Get out of my way,' Mum snapped, elbowing me aside irritably as she reached into the twin-tub washing machine with a large pair of wooden tongs and started to pull out a sodden sheet. Housekeeping was a rarity and it was clear that cleaning of any description put Mum in a foul mood. 'What are yous up to anyway?'

I didn't answer and, perhaps sensing my unusual still-ness, she stopped what she was doing and turned to look at me. I shifted nervously from one foot to the other, clenching my hands together so hard they hurt.

'I've got something to tell you,' I managed at last, swal-lowing hard.

'Well, get on with it then,' Mum answered, pushing me roughly out of her way as she wrestled with the sheet, finally managing to force one end of it between the rollers of the mangle.

'It's . . .' I stopped and took a deep breath. 'It's about Dad. About . . . about what he's been doing to me.' My voice was shaky, but suddenly I seemed to find the courage I needed, and it all started to spill out in a torrent of words.

Although doing the washing in a twin-tub was easier than having to stamp on it in the bath, as I often used to do, it wasn't like using an automatic machine today, and Mum was flushed with the effort of it. But the colour drained out of her face and she fell back against the wall in a state of shock, mumbling, 'What are we going to do now? What am I supposed to do?'

She was obviously in a complete panic, and totally oblivious to the water that was cascading over the floor from the abandoned sheet. The next thing I remember, the house seemed to be full of police asking me questions.

I'm not very clear about what happened after that, because those memories, like so many others, seem to have become sealed off in my mind behind a firmly locked door, which I'm too frightened to try to open. But I don't remember Dad coming home from the pub that day, so I assume he was picked up there by the police and then taken to prison. What I do remember, though, is that as soon as we knew he wasn't coming home, we all ran around the house wild with excitement, flinging all the windows open in a gesture of freedom and release.

Mum obviously knew that Dad lost his temper regularly – she was often on the receiving end herself – and although he would beat me to within an inch of my life, she rarely intervened. But I've thought about it a lot over the years, and however unlikely it may sound, I'm pretty sure that until that moment she had no idea that Dad was abusing me sexually as well – although maybe I just can't bear the thought that she did know. But despite her apparent indifference, and the fact that she stopped looking after us completely once she started drinking heavily, I loved her until the day she died. I'm convinced that if she'd married someone else, someone who was the opposite of my father, she'd have been a totally different person. She was a trained silver-service waitress, and used to work and have fun before she got married, but Dad bullied and abused her just like he bullied and abused me, and she simply didn't have the strength of character to fight back against him. So I'm sure that her reaction that day was one of genuine shock, and she certainly reported what I'd told her to the police.

A few days later, a social worker turned up at the house wanting to talk to us all. Mum was too drunk to make any sense, and when he suggested taking me to his office to 'have a chat', she waved her arms in what seemed to be vague agreement and I went off with him.

Once I was away from the house, the floodgates opened, and I told the social worker about the way we lived, and about how I had to do all the cleaning and cooking and look after myself and Shuggie and Alex because our parents were either too busy drinking or too drunk and indifferent to do anything for any of us. Then I told him a bit about what Dad had been doing to me, although I was too frightened to say very much, because the thought that Mum would suffer if I ever talked to anyone about it was still deeply ingrained in me.

Later, I was interviewed by four or five different people, and taken from one cheerless, grey room to another to be cross-examined until I felt as though I was the one who'd done something wrong. Someone would ask me to describe what Dad did to me, and when I told them, briefly, without going into the worst of the details, they'd say sharply, 'Are you sure that happened? You're just making it up, aren't you?'

As the minutes ticked by, I began to feel dirty, tainted by what my father did to me, and embarrassed by the unsympathetic and sometimes obviously disbelieving attitudes of the people who were interviewing me. It was hard enough to talk about it in any case, but as I sat with my head cast down, staring at my hands and twisting my fingers together in my lap, I longed for someone to say something kind to me, something that would take away the feeling that *I'd* done something wrong. But no one said anything reassuring or friendly, and the whole process did nothing to reduce the feelings of guilt that had been growing inside me for so many years.

There was talk of my going to stay with relatives, or into some sort of children's home, but I knew that I couldn't leave home just like that, because there'd be no one there to look after Shuggie and Alex. They were too young to take care of themselves, and relied on me to do everything for them. So it was agreed that we'd all have Christmas together, but that I could contact the social worker at any time if things became too difficult to cope with.

I was fully used to miserable Christmases, and to the pointlessness of making Christmas lists. The only things I hoped for each year were something to eat and enough coal to make a fire. But that year, with Dad out of the way, I was determined we were going to make the most of Christmas. I sneaked into the park on Christmas Eve and tugged and tugged at the flimsy branch of a tree until it snapped. Then I took it home, and when the boys were asleep, my sisters and I stuck it in a pot and covered it with bits of tin foil.

I'll never forget the expression on Shuggie's and Alex's faces when they woke up in the morning and saw it standing in the corner of the front room. Their eyes were as big as saucers.

'Where did it come from?' Alex asked, touching it hesitantly as though he was afraid it might disappear.

'The fairies brought it while you were asleep,' I told him.

Suddenly, he spotted the little wrapped packages under

the Christmas branch, and while he and Shuggie ripped open the couple of cheap toys and selection packs that had been bought (and stolen!) from the local shops, I brought in some sticks from the garden and set about laying a fire. Later, we made a bread-and-butter pudding and then, with our tummies full, sat round the fire playing games. Mum was drinking, as usual, but without Dad there, there weren't going to be any thrashings for the boys or sexual abuse for me, and it was the best Christmas I could ever remember.

Unfortunately, while Dad was in jail on remand, Mum started hitting the bottle even harder, maybe partly because she blamed herself for what had been happening to me and realized she'd let me down. Then, apparently out of the blue, she suddenly changed her attitude and refused to believe that Dad had done anything wrong. I found out later that she had retracted the statement she'd made to the police. Unable to cope with a house full of stress and arguments, my sister Mary decided to leave, and she went to stay in a hostel.

Mary had always done well at school, and once she got away from the house and had some help from the social services, she finally had time to study and concentrate on getting her life together. I could see that it was a good thing for her, and I was glad that she was being given the opportunity to make a fresh start.

But Mum reacted to her leaving by starting to beat us in a way she'd never done before. The sexual abuse may have stopped, but it began to seem as though my body was always going to be covered in bruises and I was never going to be free of living in fear. Social workers came to the house a couple of times after Christmas, but they didn't seem to think it was anything out of the ordinary that Mum was drunk, and a few weeks later in the new year, one of them offered to take her and my older brother up to the jail to visit Dad.

It wasn't until many years later, when I read the social work reports, that I discovered Dad had strongly denied the accusations I'd made against him and had insisted that everything I'd said about him had been made up. But – just in case he didn't get away with that lie – he also apparently told some story about suffering from blackouts when he'd been drinking, and claimed that if the reported incidents *had* occurred, they must have done so while he was unconscious. I don't know whether anyone believed him. You'd have thought that if he *had* been suffering from blackouts on a daily basis, which sometimes must have lasted for hours while he sexually abused me, someone would have made sure he had the medical investigations and treatment he so clearly needed.

After the social worker had taken Mum to visit Dad in jail, they went to see him again, and I think it was on that occasion that Dad apparently told the social worker he didn't want us to have to go through the trauma of giving evidence against him in court – which was pretty rich coming from someone who'd made sure that every single day of our young lives had been deeply traumatic.

Then, one evening, a few weeks after Dad had been taken away from the house, Mum got drunk and went completely crazy, beating me so badly that I thought my legs were going to snap in two. She was like someone demented, and I eventually hit her back just to get her off me. That was when I realized I simply couldn't take it any more. Was this what plucking up the courage to tell Mum about what Dad was doing to me had led to – being free from the sexual abuse, but still being physically attacked whenever Mum was drunk, which was basically every day?

Audrey tried to comfort me as I crouched on the floor beside my bed. 'I can't stay here,' I sobbed. 'She's going to kill me.'

Mum had already sunk into a deep, drunken, coma-like sleep, so there was no fear of waking her. But, even so, we whispered as we woke up Alex and Shuggie, crept out of the front door and then ran up the road to our aunt's house.

The next morning, Audrey and I went to the social worker's office to tell him what had happened to me, and I showed him the black and purple bruises that completely covered my legs. It was obvious I couldn't go back to live with Mum, so the social worker took us all back to our aunt's house, and although she had four children of her own, she agreed to keep us there for a few days while something else was sorted out for us.

After the social workers had dropped us off at our aunt's, they went round to visit Mum and found her in a bad state, with clear signs of her heavy drinking bout of the night before. Mum apparently admitted that she'd hit me, although she said that my behaviour had warranted it, and that she was finding the whole situation very difficult to deal with. She agreed to go with the social workers to my aunt's house to talk to us – although it didn't change anything, because we were determined not to go home unless Mum stopped drinking, which I suppose we must have realized wasn't actually going to happen.

Audrey and I shared a bedroom with our cousins at our aunt's house, and we were all crammed in like sardines in a tin. But it was a happy house, and we felt safe. Sleeping there was a completely new experience for us, because there was always a fire burning in the bedroom grate, which meant that we didn't have to pile clothes on to the bed to try to keep out the bitter cold like we did at home, and we fell asleep each night feeling warm and comfortable.

One night, as Audrey and I were lying in bed sleepily,

clinging to each other like two lost souls, my final, half-formed thought before I fell into a deep, untroubled sleep was that all the brutal misery and unhappiness I'd suffered for so long might be coming to an end at last. Perhaps we had a future after all.

The next morning, we were playing in the street, running and shouting with all the other kids, when my aunt appeared at her front door and called us in. My heart skipped a beat when I saw a social worker standing in the kitchen, and I edged closer to Audrey in an instinctive and unconscious search for her support.

'The social workers are going up to visit your Dad,' my aunt told us, 'and they want to take you with them. So go and have a wash and tidy yourselves up a bit. You look like something the cat spat out.'

My heart sank, but I followed Audrey up to the bathroom obediently and splashed water on my face, and although we didn't actually say anything to each other, I was sure Audrey was thinking the same as I was: going up to the prison to see my father was the last thing in the world either of us wanted to do. Being at my auntie's house over the last few days, it had felt as though the lid had been taken off a pressure cooker and all the steam that had been building up for so long was gradually being allowed to escape. I could go to bed at night, turn over on to my side and go to sleep, rather than having to lie anxiously on my back, watching the light around the door for signs of the dark shadow that meant my father had stopped outside my room and was about to turn the door handle and come in.

But we were used to doing whatever we were told, so we tidied ourselves up as well as we could and went downstairs again.

After waiting a few minutes at the prison, with me fighting against the familiar feeling of cold fear that was rising up inside me, we were told that we could go in and see Dad. Standing tense and rigid with the effort of controlling my shaking body, I hung back from the table, concentrating my attention on wiping my shoes carefully on my socks, until I suddenly realized that Dad was talking to me.

'I said "Come here," Lizzie,' he ordered, glaring at me from across the table.

I tried to swallow the hard little lump that had lodged in my throat. Surely he couldn't do anything to me here? Not in a prison with people all around? I edged a little closer, until his finger was pointing almost directly into my face.

'What the fuck do you think you're playing at?' he hissed at me angrily. 'Deserting your mum and leaving her to cope on her own. Get yourself back home. And you can tell the solicitor that the things you said about me were lies, that you made them up.'

His voice sounded harsh, and I could feel his breath on my face as he almost spat the words at me. He was right, though. We shouldn't have left Mum to try to manage on her own. The old feeling of guilt washed over me again.

Too frightened to look Dad in the face, I glanced away, and with tears pricking my eyes at the unfairness of it all, whispered, 'Yes, Dad. OK.'

I'd already been with a social worker to see Dad's solicitor, who'd apparently wanted to verify my story but had taken the opportunity to explain how difficult it would be to make the charges stick. I felt under a huge amount of pressure to give in – after all, who would believe me over Dad? My visit to see him in prison had shown me that, despite being locked up, he was still the boss, and he would always be able to control me, wherever he was.

Back at our aunt's house, I went up to the bedroom to pack the few meagre possessions I had with me. But when I went downstairs again, Audrey was nowhere to be seen.

'She's decided to stay here with your aunt,' the social worker told me. 'She doesn't want to go home.'

I was stunned. Surely they must be mistaken? Was I really going to be left to deal with it all on my own? But they hadn't got it wrong: I really was the only one going home. I don't think I ever really got over the sense of hurt and abandonment I felt that day. I couldn't trust anyone.

So, reluctantly, I moved back in with my mum. I hadn't been back home for long when one of my relatives came to the house and kicked the shit out of me, knocking me into every corner of the back bedroom, for hitting my mum. It would have been funny, if only I'd still had the ability to laugh. After all I'd had to put up with, all the beatings and abuse, the bruises and broken bones, the cruel neglect by my almost permanently drunk parents, no one in the family had ever intervened. But hitting my mum – a hopeless, and now often aggressive, alcoholic – so that I could escape her vicious attack was unacceptable. *Now* a family member was prepared to step in. It was a weird logic, but one that I just had to live with.

At around the same time, Mum started to feel ill. I thought it was the drink and didn't really give it too much thought until she was rushed to hospital and found to be suffering from a serious kidney infection. With Mary living in the hostel and Audrey still staying with our aunt, I was left to look after Shuggie and Alex on my own. It wasn't as if I wasn't used to cooking and cleaning and taking care of them; the only difference Mum's absence really made was that it meant there was no one in the house getting drunk and hitting us. On our first night alone, we stayed up late to watch a horror movie on TV, and then sat, shell-shocked and feeling considerably less brave than we'd thought we were, while the final credits rolled.

'Right,' I said after a few moments, getting up off the sofa and clearing my throat to cover the slight quaver in my voice. 'You boys check that the back windows are locked and I'll check the front ones.'

Alex and Shuggie went into the kitchen together, and I pulled back the living-room curtains – and almost died of fright. There, staring in at me, was some guy with a knife, who was quite obviously trying to force open the window. For a few seconds I was too shocked to react, but then, as the panic started rising up inside me, it pushed out a hoarse scream, and the boys came running back into the room.

Presumably the guy was someone who knew that Dad was in prison and Mum was in hospital, and the last thing he was expecting was to find kids alone in the house. He must have been almost as shocked as we were, and he took to his heels and fled across the fields.

Grabbing the mop, I started banging on the ceiling, until we eventually heard the sounds of someone moving around in the flat above and then footsteps running down the stairs. I flung open the front door and we clamoured to explain to the woman from upstairs what had happened, and then all rushed back to the window.

Having recovered from his initial surprise and realizing that he didn't actually have much to fear from a bunch of kids, the guy had stopped running and was watching us from across the road. Fortunately, seeing that there was an adult with us was enough to send him off again, and he turned and ran off across the field, while we watched in relief until he was out of sight. And that was the end of our staying home alone.

When Mary heard what had happened, she contacted social services, and the social worker insisted that we should be farmed out to various relatives. I was sent to stay with one of my uncles and his wife, who gave me another taste of family life and a bit of respite from the daily grind of running a house and looking after two small boys.

Mum was in hospital for several days, feeling very ill and in a lot of pain, and it turned out that the poison from her kidney infection had started to spread throughout her body. She was lucky to survive. Then, when she came home again, so did we, and the social services seemed pretty much to lose interest in us after that, and we were more or less left to muddle through and get on with things.

I sometimes wondered where Dad would go when he'd served his time and was released from jail. I hoped that it was far away and that someone would make sure that we were protected from him, because I didn't think there was a lock in the world that would keep him out of the house if he decided – as I knew he would – to come and teach me a lesson for snitching on him. But, in the event,

I was worrying about the wrong things. We weren't going to need strong locks to defend us against Dad, because he was released home, and he came back to live in the same house as me – the child who had accused him of sexual and physical abuse. The child who had put him in prison.

Why did anyone think that that was all right?

Chapter Six

On the day Dad was released from prison, he sat in the living room sobbing as though his heart would break and begging Mum to forgive him.

'You *have* to believe me,' he said through his tears. 'I swear I'll never lay a finger on the kids again. Never!' And then he described the perfect life they were going to live together in the future.

I sat looking from him to Mum and back again in disbelief. Eventually, I couldn't hold my tongue any longer and blurted out, 'Don't! Please, Mum. You cannae do this!'

But, once again, he'd managed to fool her.

'Your dad's right, Lizzie,' she told me, her eyes filling with tears. 'We need to try and make this work.'

Yeah, and there goes *my* life down the Swannee again, I thought bitterly.

That night, Mum and Dad got drunk together, and everything was back to normal. Within a few days, Dad dragged me into my bedroom by my hair, leering into my face and taunting me, saying, 'Ha ha, you're not such a smart-arse now, are you?' and then left me shaking and defeated, knowing exactly how my life was going to be from then on.

I could never relax for a single moment, I was always on red alert; and life got steadily worse – which I think most people would have known was inevitable. Dad had always been an angry man, and anyone could have guessed that he'd be even angrier after spending time in prison; and perhaps he felt he needed to reassert his control over us. But, whatever the reason, the beatings and abuse became more brutal and viciously soul-destroying than ever before.

Night after night, I'd lie in bed tense with listening, the familiar knot twisting itself around my stomach, until I heard him shouting, swearing and kicking things as he staggered down the road on his way home from the pub. After a few minutes spent scrabbling at the front door trying to fit his key in the lock, he and Mum would lurch drunkenly into the flat, making a poor job of holding each other up. Then I'd hear him throw Mum on to their bed to sleep it off, and I'd shut my eyes tightly and try to flatten myself into invisibility under the bed covers, praying silently, 'Please, God. Not tonight. Please. Just let me have one night without this. Don't make me go through it again.' But within seconds, my bedroom door would fly back against the wall with a thud, and my father would be standing there, swaying gently in the doorway as he fumbled to undo the zip on his trousers.

Pinned to the bed by the dead weight of his body, I could barely breathe for the stench of him, and I'd soon be soaked in the mixture of alcohol and sweat that oozed from his pores. Usually, he was silent as he humped and pummelled me, and I'd lie underneath him with hot tears dripping into my hair, praying for it to be over and trying not to move or do anything that might prolong my torment. Sometimes he'd mumble and mutter, 'Do you like that, Lizzie? Oh, you're liking that, aren't you?' until I longed to cover my ears with my hands and scream.

Then, when he'd finally suffocated the last ounce of resistance out of me, he'd stand up, pull up his zip and leave me to cry myself to sleep, so that I could wake up the next morning knowing that I had to get through another, almost identically miserable day.

The fact was that Dad did whatever he wanted to do. Everything was *his* choice; whatever happened was entirely up to him – and that included whatever happened to me. I was just there for the taking. He used to make me stand outside his bedroom door and then shout out my name, summoning me into his room. As I waited to hear 'Lizzie!' bellowed through the door, I would stand there whimpering like a terrified dog, shaking and so frightened that I'd sometimes lose control and wet myself. My heart would be breaking with sadness, and it seemed at the time that things were as bad as they could possibly be. But I look back now and realize how much worse they could have been, if I hadn't been a late developer (my periods didn't start until I was fifteen).

After Dad came out of prison, I learned a very important lesson: no one was ever going to help me, and even if someone told me that it was safe to tell my secret because they'd protect me, that wasn't ever going to be true. I felt that it was entirely my responsibility to look after Shuggie and Alex and try to protect them from my father's violent beatings. I'd always clung desperately to the belief that, although Dad might be able to break my bones, he could never break my spirit. When I read the social worker's report years later, I couldn't believe what had been written just after Dad came out of prison: it was stated that I seemed well and that I appeared not to be finding it difficult having my father back home, that I had somehow forgotten about what had happened.

Can they really have had so little imagination, so little understanding? Did they really think that a man who'd just spent three months in prison for physically and sexually assaulting me, and who had basically been sent to prison as the result of statements I'd made about him, would be treating me well? A man who kept the front door locked and the key in his pocket or under his pillow when he was in bed, and who was often so drunk when social workers visited the family at home that he had passed out and the children had to whisper through the letterbox?

Even today, when I read that statement in the social worker's report, it makes me want to weep. It's as though I'm detached from my old self and I feel a desperate sadness, and an almost overpowering anger at the thought of how badly I was let down and left to suffer at the hands of my tyrant of a father, a man without the ability to love and without any sense of humanity.

The social worker also wrote in a report about me: 'She also goes babysitting for her auntie, who lives nearby. She gets well paid for this and she appears to be never short of money. Her home and bedroom are very comfortable and there is evidence she is well provided for materially. There is a music centre in her bedroom which she appears to get much enjoyment from.'

In fact, my 'music centre' was an old reel-to-reel tape recorder that someone had given me. I loved listening to music, and I'd taped some of her records and used to sit in my room playing them over and over again. And as for the babysitting . . .

I used to love babysitting, but Dad only let me do it so that he could take the money off me to spend on drink. As well as my auntie, there was another lady I babysat for. She was always really kind to me, and she'd sometimes buy me little presents, I think because she knew that I had to hand over to my Dad the money she gave me. But it wasn't the money that mattered to me. What was important was the means of escape that babysitting gave me, and the opportunity to sit in peace for a while without having to keep one eye on the door and listen for my father's key in the lock.

The house where I babysat was in the next close to ours, and I used to pretend that I lived there. Although I knew that my dad was sitting drinking just around the corner, I'd imagine for a few hours that I never had to go home again; that I would never have to sit and wait for my dad to force himself on me when he got back from the pub again; and that I was never again going to be punched and kicked for some imagined infringement of his rules.

The girl I babysat for was a little treasure, and it was a lovely home, and a huge treat for me to be somewhere nice for a while. I'd sometimes potter around after the little girl had gone to bed and do some cleaning, trying to make things nice for her mum when she got back. And keeping busy helped me to block out the harshness of reality and immerse myself in another, make-believe world where everything was clean and orderly and people were kind to each other. Sometimes, when I babysat, one of the girl's friends would be there as well, and sometimes my friend Jacky would babysit with me, and after we'd played with the girls and tucked them up in bed, we'd watch television together.

One night, Jacky and I were babysitting for the girl and one of her friends and I'd just put the kettle on to start making tea and toast for the little ones before they went to bed when there was a noise at the front door. But before I'd even managed to get my backside out of the chair, someone started thumping and banging, hard enough to burst the door off its hinges. The two little girls stared at me, their eyes wide with terror, and I turned to look at Jacky. We were both frozen to the spot, but I realized that the little ones were looking to us to be the adults. We couldn't let them see that we were scared too.

'It's all right,' I whispered, as calmly as I could. 'You just have to keep very quiet while I phone the police. Don't worry. Everything's going to be all right. I promise.'

Suddenly, there was a loud metallic clatter as the flap of the letterbox flew up and a drunken voice started yelling obscenities through the opening. It felt as though someone was standing on my chest, and I had to wait a moment for my heart to start beating again – because it was a voice I knew only too well. It was my dad.

Putting the phone receiver back down as quietly as I could, I almost flung the little girls behind the couch that stood across the corner of the room, out of sight of the front door, and Jacky dived on top of them. Then, once they were safely out of the way, I stood near the window, with the idea of waiting for someone to pass by outside, so that I could shout out to them for help and tell them to go my gran's house, which was just around the corner, and get my uncle. I knew that my uncle would soon sort it all out and make sure that the girls were safe, and that Dad wouldn't dare do anything if he was there.

But no one passed by the window and, gradually, Dad's shouts started to lose their force. Then, as I was just beginning to allow myself to hope that we might have fooled him into thinking there was no one in the house, the kettle came to the boil with a loud click.

A second later, the door came crashing in and Dad burst into the hallway, bellowing with rage: 'I knew you were in there, you wee bastard.' Then he crept like a panther along the hall, glancing into every room, and I almost fell behind the couch in my haste to join the others, my heart racing as I used my body to try to cover the children.

Dad continued to search the house, keeping up a constant barrage of shouting and swearing, and I was sure that, if he stopped for a moment, he'd be able to hear the sound of my heart thumping painfully in my chest. But although my whole body was trembling with fear, I managed to smile weakly at the children and cuddle them, while praying that my dad would give up the search and go away.

Suddenly, a terrified little whimper escaped from behind the sofa and, instantly, he was there, towering above us and, to my horror, clutching a hatchet. He reached over and tapped me on the head with its handle, roaring, 'Out of there, you bitch. So where are the boys hiding?'

Before I could answer, he grabbed me by the hair and started dragging me from room to room, waving the hatchet like a man possessed and smashing everything in his path, tearing things out of cupboards and wardrobes, looking for the boys he was convinced were hiding somewhere in the house. I'd seen this madness in him before, many times, and I knew there was no point trying to put up a fight.

Finally, he dragged me back into the living room, and turned on Jacky so abruptly that she almost fainted with shock, shouting, 'Get out! Get away home.' She sprinted out of the smashed front door like a gazelle, as though the devil himself were snapping at her heels.

Then, still holding me by my hair, Dad pulled me down two flights of stairs and into the street, lashing out with the occasional kick and punch until we reached our flat, the two girls following us like a pair of lost lambs.

As soon as we were inside our front door, he beat the living daylights out of me – with the girls standing there watching, clutching each other and crying pitifully – and he was still thrashing me when the little girl's mother arrived, threw me a pitying glance, hastily grabbed both girls and took them away. Having seen what my dad was capable of, she must have decided not to risk pressing charges, as he was never even questioned about the damage he had caused to her house, let alone arrested.

The beating and sexual abuse continued for hours that night, while my mum lay drunk in another room. After throwing me against the wall over and over again, and then punching and kicking me, my dad forced himself on me so hard it felt as though I was being torn apart from the inside. Then, just as I thought I was going to die, he stopped, zipped up his trousers, gave me a final, half-hearted punch, and left me to sob myself into a fitful, exhausted sleep.

The next day, I couldn't walk. But of course there was no question of being allowed to go to the doctor or a hospital, and so my fractures were just left to heal themselves. It was weeks before the bruises had faded from my face and body enough for me to go to school again.

It must have taken days for that poor woman to get her lovely home back to normal and, understandably, she never asked me to babysit again. But, in a way, that was a relief, because every time I thought about what those wee girls had witnessed and how terrified they must have been, I felt sick. At least I wouldn't be responsible for their safety any more.

As I got older, Dad's paranoia about me even talking to boys got more and more out of control, and I knew that one of the lessons he was teaching me was that I wasn't to get any ideas about going with boys. But, ironically, I was a tomboy anyway and – quite apart from the fact that the experience I'd already had of sex would probably be enough to put anyone off it for life – the thought of having a boyfriend had never even entered my head.

My fear of my father was so intense that it seemed to have its roots down in the depths of my very soul. It's an extraordinary feeling to be so afraid of someone that you freeze on the spot when you hear their voice, like a terrified rabbit caught in headlights and unable to do anything to avoid its terrible and inevitable fate. You hold your breath, and can't move or speak. Then, suddenly, you're breathing at 1,000 breaths a second and your heart's thumping so fast and so hard that you think you can actually hear it crashing against your ribcage. But however much you try to tell yourself to calm down, there's nothing you can do, because the fear gets hold of you and overwhelms you, and you completely lose control of your body.

Even to this day, a certain smell or someone coming into a room unexpectedly can set off the same reaction, and I go from sensible adult to babbling, incoherent child within a wisp of a second. And it's a fear that never goes away. I know that for the rest of my life I'll always jump with fright in response to certain triggers. For example, even now, if someone is sitting beside me and they move suddenly, or raise their hand for some reason, I react as though they're about to hit me. I just can't ever relax. However calm I might seem to be, there's a tiny dynamo whirring away inside me, and my body is always wound up and ready to leap into action to try to protect myself.

Although I was too frightened of Dad to do anything except submit to his vicious attacks and sexual assaults, some of the neighbours began to give him a hard time after he came out of prison, and people would stare at him in the street. For us, though, it meant having to live with the thought that everyone might be gossiping about what had happened. I used to feel really ashamed when I walked past all the old biddies, because although I imagined them whispering 'poor wee soul', I also felt they must be thinking that it was all my fault and that I should have spoken out sooner. But Dad had me terrified of my own shadow, and I realize now that probably no one was actually blaming me, because even though I always used to feel that I was somehow responsible for everything bad that ever happened, I was really only a child.

The social workers came to the house about a week

after my dad was released from prison, and wrote in a report following that visit, 'The strain on him [my dad] has been quite considerable whilst being at home, not so much from the family – they seem to have accepted him quite readily back into the home – but from the neighbours.'

It's hard to credit the thought that anyone had any sympathy for my dad – although obviously there were people who didn't, because one evening, when Dad had been out drinking, a gang of local boys attacked him and beat him up. Shortly after that, he and my older brother Francis packed up their things and left for London.

Chapter Seven

After Dad and Francis left, Mum's drinking carried on, but with ever more alarming intensity. She did seem to be trying to do her best for us, and she put her early waitress experience to good use for a while and went to work at a local hotel. I hadn't seen her laugh for a long time, but she'd come home from work with steaks stuffed down her trousers, and she'd pull them out with a flourish and announce proudly, 'Look what I've got for tea!' It was a happy time in some ways. However, she started becoming more and more aggressive towards us, and would eventually thrash us without even pretending to have an excuse. One good thing was that at least I didn't have to endure the sexual abuse as well and, without Dad there, Mum was more prepared to ask for help from the social services.

Sometimes, when Mum was lying in a drunken stupor, we'd sneak out of the house for a while, and one day I somehow managed to get some money to go ice-skating with some other kids. I was really excited, and elated at the thought that perhaps, with Dad gone, I might be able to start making friends who I could do normal things with.

But it turned out to be just another disappointing, deeply hurtful experience, and not at all the exciting adventure I'd hoped it would be.

I can't remember now, but perhaps no one actually asked me to go with them, and I was just tagging along, because they left me on my own at the ice-skating rink, skating off together and laughing whenever I went near them. Although I felt rejected and humiliated, I was determined not to give in, and I battled on, pretending that I was part of the group.

As soon as the skating session was over, I shoved my aching feet back into my shoes and rushed after the other kids to catch the train home. But, as I ran down the stairs at the train station, I tripped and fell, badly spraining my ankle. The pain seemed to shoot right through my body as I got to my feet and tried to hobble after them, and I could see that my ankle was already swollen and starting to turn blue. But I was used to pain, and I simply refused to let go of the illusion that, for once in my life, I had some friends to go out with, however reluctant and unfriendly they might actually be.

I did get the chance to be a regular kid for a while, though, because I started going to the youth club at the local church, where kids of all ages and from all sorts of backgrounds messed around together and had fun. There, for the first time, I seemed to be accepted.

* * *

A few months after he had left home, Dad was arrested in London for pimping and running a prostitution racket. He was sent to Pentonville Prison to await trial, but when he was granted bail, he and Francis came home – and our brief period of relative calm was over.

As it turned out, one of the key witnesses in the case was found dead, so Dad never went to trial and was free to settle down again with his family – and the nightmare continued.

He'd sometimes rape me three or even four times a day, and if he'd been up all night drinking, he'd often drag me back into my bedroom before I left the house for school. There was nothing that was out of bounds as far as he was concerned – oral sex, anal sex, forcing me to touch him – and he wasn't afraid to touch me in front of other people. He'd make some joke and grope between my legs or touch my breasts and say, 'Your wee buds are growing now.' No one seemed to see anything wrong in it, but I hated it and would try to pull away, feeling humiliated and resentful.

One night, I was woken up by the sound of banging and thumping. It seemed to be coming from the stairs on the other side of my bedroom wall, which went up to the flat on the floor above us. Then, just as abruptly as it had started, the noise stopped. I swung my legs over the side of my bed, tiptoed across my room and started to open my bedroom door. At that moment, someone grabbed the door knob on the other side so I couldn't turn it, and

I heard my dad saying gruffly, 'No. Get back in your room. You're not getting out.' Puzzled, but still sleepy, I climbed back into bed, and it wasn't until the next morning that I found out what had happened.

Apparently, the man who lived upstairs had been drinking at our house and had left to go home, but as he tried to put his key in his front door, he'd fallen all the way back down the stairs again, banging his head against the wall that divided the landing from my bedroom. That was the sound that had woken me – and by the time I heard it, he was already lying dead on our doorstep.

We didn't really know what other people's lives were like, so I didn't realize that not everyone's houses were full of people drinking and having sex, and there were some things I just assumed happened to everyone, however much my instincts were shocked and repulsed by them. For example, one night, when some of Dad's mates were drinking at the house, I slipped out of my room as quietly as I could to go to the bathroom and came across Dad having sex with a drunken woman I had never seen before. I turned and rushed back to my bedroom, the horrible sounds they were making still echoing in my head. Throwing myself onto my bed, hot tears of shame spilling down my cheeks I gripped my pillow around my head so tightly I thought I was going to suffocate, but I could still hear their grunts and groans and the sound of the bed banging against the wall. I lay there feeling physically sick and praying, 'Please, God, let me fall asleep now so that I don't have to listen to this any more.'

As far as my dad was concerned, everyone was there for the using. That was the way he lived his life: nothing was sacred to him. There always seemed to be willing participants, although they may have been so drunk that they didn't really know what they were doing, and he often had more than one woman in his bed at a time.

I was fourteen when I started working in the kitchens at a local hotel, washing dishes at weekends and in the evenings. The work added to the terrible exhaustion I already felt by the time I'd got home from school, done my homework, fed the boys and got everything ready for the next day. After I'd been at the hotel for a while, the chef started teaching me to cook, and he and his wife were very kind to me – and there were precious few people in my life at that time who I could say that about. In fact, they were so easy to talk to that there were several occasions when I almost told them what was happening at home, but in the end I just couldn't bring myself to do it.

There was still always that part of me that believed everything was somehow my fault; I imagine it's the same for any child on the receiving end of violence and sexual abuse. The paradox was that, if I ever found someone who seemed to like me and feel sympathetic towards me, I'd long to talk to them about what was going on, but I thought that, if I did, they'd see what a disgusting, horrible person I really was and stop liking me. I was trapped in a vicious circle, and I suppose that's partly why people get away with abusing children – sometimes for years – and why so many abused children keep their terrible secret to themselves.

Every Friday night, I'd hand my wages from the hotel over to my dad so that he could add the money to his drinks pot for the weekend. One Friday I wasn't in the kitchen when they brought round the wages, and when I got home that night without the money, Dad hit the roof. It had been his constant threat throughout my childhood that if any of us told anyone about what he did to us, he'd make sure that Mum suffered for it. And if I'd ever had any doubt about whether he meant it or not, it disappeared that night.

He forced me to sit and watch while he kicked my mum from one side of the room to the other, punching and beating her until her face was so cut and swollen that it was unrecognizable. I was shouting and sobbing and begging him to stop, but he just ignored me, until eventually he turned and shouted into my face, 'So now you know what will happen if you *ever* come home without your wages again.'

Mum was lying on the floor moaning, her face bloated and bloody and wet with tears. It turned out that Dad had broken some of her ribs as well, but it was her face that haunted me after that; *that* was the image that came into my mind whenever Dad threatened to hurt her if I told anyone what he was doing to us. I made sure that I never did come home without my wages again.

Dad was always sending Mum round to the houses of other members of her family to try to get money. They knew it was for drink so, whatever story she told them, they'd refuse to give her any, and Dad would beat her when she came home with nothing. I'd sit in my room trying to block out the sound of her voice as she pleaded with him: 'I'm sorry. I'm sorry. They wouldn't give me anything.' But there was no blocking the sound of her pathetic sobs, or of her cries of pain as he punched and kicked her.

I was in my room one day when I heard a sound I didn't recognize, and as I strained to listen, I realized it was the sound of muffled screaming. I went into the living room to investigate. Dad was sitting alone on the couch, with his arms folded and a drink beside him, watching TV. I stood nervously in the doorway for a few moments, but there was no one in the room making the weird, muted screams I could still hear. I went into the kitchen, but there was no one there either. Puzzled, I came out again into the hallway, and as I did so, the screams seemed to be a bit louder. I opened the hall cupboard, but it was empty, and so was the bathroom. By this time I was completely bewildered, and I stood again in the hallway, wondering where on earth the sound could be coming from. Then I went back into the living room, and my dad was still sitting watching TV, smirking slightly but apparently oblivious to the noise I could hear.

The only place I hadn't searched was a cupboard behind where my dad was sitting, and walking towards it, I saw Mum's legs sticking out from under his chair. Horrified, I realized that she was trapped by the neck, with her head under the chair, and she was slowly choking to death while he sat, calmly indifferent, kicking her casually on the legs from time to time.

Although I was terrified of what Dad would do to me, I knew my mum was going to die if I didn't do something. So, before he had time to react, I lunged towards him, grabbed him by the arms and tried to drag him out of his chair. I'd normally never have dared lay a finger on him, so he was taken completely by surprise, and he leapt to his feet in fury, effing and blinding and laying into me with his fists. As he stood up, I just had time to kick the chair off Mum, and as soon as the pressure of his weight was lifted off her, she managed to wriggle free and run out of the room, coughing and choking. Distracted for a moment, Dad loosened his grip on me, and I took my opportunity and fled after her.

Out of breath and shaking with fear, I sat with Mum on the floor in my room, our backs against the door and our feet braced on the side of the bed as we waited for Dad to start trying to kick his way in. But he'd already straightened his chair, picked up his whisky bottle and turned his attention back to his TV programme.

I'd been playing truant from school for quite a while, and whenever I did go to classes, I'd just sit daydreaming, looking at the other girls and wondering what their lives were like and if they had to do the things that I had to do. I'd always felt an outsider at school, like I was cut off from everyone behind glass, just watching, but at least I was relatively safe there. I used to dread going home every day. I'd started arriving at school in the mornings in time to register and collect my free lunch ticket, and then going off to a friend's house. Her mum would be at work, and I think I spent some of the happiest hours of my entire childhood sitting in my friend's bedroom listening to records. I'd get back to school in time to eat my lunch, register for afternoon lessons and disappear again.

Hugh did really well at school and Alex was always very clever academically too and he's brilliant at maths. But I wanted my childhood. I was spending my time in the evenings and at weekends working in the hotel kitchen, or cooking, scrubbing and cleaning at home, being forced to take on the roles of wife, mother and housekeeper, and I felt as though my childhood was slipping away from me, that I was completely missing out on it. The only way I could manage to grab a bit of it back was by stealing time off school.

I was always there for school dinners, though, because they were the only proper meals I ever had. I used to eat as much as I could to try to fill up my tummy for as long as possible. One day, I went up for seconds of caramel cake and custard, which was my favourite, and just after I'd been served, they ran out. When I brought my plate back to the table, a girl who hadn't managed to get any stuck her finger in it and said, 'If I'm not getting any, you're not.' I pushed my plate away and left the dining room without a word. Although it may seem like a small incident, hardly worth mentioning to most people, I could have cried with disappointment, and I wondered bitterly if she'd have done the same thing if she'd known it was the only food I'd get that day.

Eventually, my poor school attendance began to be noticed, and a social worker came to the house one day to talk to my parents about it. I also had to go and see the headmaster, and he asked me for an explanation. But I didn't have an explanation – at least, none that I could tell him about, or probably even fully understand myself.

I couldn't have put into words how I felt, but I think I simply couldn't cope with life any more. My need for some time and space to myself had become so intense that it could sometimes send me into a state of panic, and there was simply no other way for me to get it other than by truanting. Looking back now, I can see that it probably seemed to the headmaster as though I was just refusing to give him an explanation out of awkwardness, and I think that's what made him angry. If only he'd known the true horror I was having to deal with.

After that, I stopped truanting for a couple of weeks, but then I started again: I *had* to have time to myself, and it was the only way I was ever going to get any. I got away with it for about two more years, probably because no one really cared enough to look into it much. The truth was right there in front of anyone who cared to see it. I can't help but think it couldn't have been very hard to work out that my truanting might have something to do with the fact that I was always so ready to use my fists, or that my father had been sent to prison for 'lewd and libidinous behaviour', or even that my brothers and I were constantly covered with bruises. It felt like it was easier for everyone to ignore what was going on and not try to get to the bottom of it, because at least if I was out of the way, I wasn't causing anyone any trouble.

Then, one day, I was out with a friend and we were

caught stealing from a shop and taken to the police station. We'd stolen make-up, amongst other things. I ask you – make-up! The last thing I wanted was attention from boys, so what the hell did I want with make-up?

At the police station, although, obviously, I knew I was in trouble, for the first time in my life I had the strange sensation of feeling safe. As long as I was surrounded by police officers, it felt as though no one could get at me, and I begged them not to take me home – ever.

I kept pleading with anyone who would listen: 'Please don't take me home. I'll go anywhere; I'll do anything you want me to do. Please, please. I cannae go home.'

You'd think my desperation might have rung some sort of alarm bell, but I suppose they thought I was just afraid of the trouble I'd get into with my parents for stealing and missing school. So they told me not to be silly, bundled me into a car and took me home.

By the time the car pulled up outside our house, I'd lost the will to resist and was sitting dejected and silently crying, ready to accept whatever came next. Of course, Mum and Dad acted like any normal parents would and expressed shock at what I'd done. Dad was particularly apologetic and polite to the police officers.

'I'm really sorry you've had all this trouble, officers,' he said in a respectful voice. 'It's not like Lizzie to do something like that. She's usually a good girl, so I'm really surprised at her. But don't worry. I'll have a good talk with her and sort it out. Thank you for all your help, and for bringing her home.'

As the front door closed behind them, I started to edge my way down the hall towards my bedroom. But I knew it was useless trying to escape.

'Elizabeth!' Dad roared from behind me. 'What the fuck have you been doing?'

His fingers twisted in my hair as he dragged me back up the hallway and struck the first blow across my face. As my body slammed into the opposite wall, I tried to cover my head with my arms, terrified that this might be the day when he finally killed me, or at least seriously damaged my brain.

What seemed like hours later, I lay curled up on my bed, too exhausted even to cry any more. I longed to drift off into a deep, dreamless sleep that would last until my bruises had faded and the terrible pains that were stabbing through every part of my body had gone. But before long I heard the bedroom door open, and I froze, holding my breath, my eyes tightly shut. My father lay down on the bed beside me and started running his hands over my bruises. I tried to turn my head away but his fingers gripped my jaw and dug into my cheeks like rods of iron, and I knew it was pointless trying to resist as his mouth closed over mine and he forced his tongue between my lips, one hand already working its way inside my pants.

'Concentrate,' I told myself. 'Think about something else.' And I tried to imagine myself anywhere other than where I was, in my bedroom, lying on my bed while my father forced himself on me, breathing his foul breath into my face and whispering, 'You like that, don't you, Lizzie? You like it when Daddy does that to you, don't you?'

My father could keep up his assaults – both physical and sexual – for hours at a time. But at last it was over, and he staggered to his feet, zipped up his trousers and said, 'Now get yourself cleaned up. And don't you *ever* get brought home by the police again.' And, with that, he turned his back on me and left the room.

After he'd closed the door, I lay on the bed weeping silent tears, the sour taste of alcohol and stale tobacco making me retch, and then edged my way painfully to the bathroom to try to scrub the stench of my father off my body. Looking at myself in the mirror, I wondered what it was that I kept doing that made my father treat me the way he did, and how many more of his assaults I could take. It was a question I never seemed to get any closer to answering, although, of course, on this occasion it was clear that he was punishing me not so much for truanting and shoplifting – after all, stealing was a way of life for my dad – but for getting caught. Wiping my tears with the back of my hand so that Shuggie and Alex wouldn't see them, I went to the kitchen to try to find something to cook for our dinner.

Chapter Eight

Alex and Shuggie weren't angels by any means, and they both went through stages in their lives when they were a bit wild, but they were good people, whereas my older brother, Francis, ended up serving a prison sentence for culpable homicide.

Dad was drunk the day the police came to the house to arrest Francis – although that's a fact that doesn't really even need to be mentioned, as I don't think a single day ever passed when Dad wasn't drunk. He was storming around the house shouting and swearing, while Francis just kept saying over and over again, 'I'm sorry, Mum. I'm sorry.'

After the police had taken Francis away, Dad was in a blind rage – not angry with my brother for what he'd done but furious that he hadn't been able to stop the police arresting him. Dad wasn't used to other people taking control and, that day, his anger seemed to reach a new level.

I was so frightened that I was scarcely able to breathe, and I crept into my room and curled up in a trembling ball on my bed, trying to shut out the sound of Dad's voice. After a few minutes, my bedroom door flew open and I leapt to my feet and cowered against the wall as Dad came bursting in. He dragged me back on to the bed, gripping my wrist so tightly that I could feel the blood pounding in the veins of my arm, and raped me over and over again until I thought he was going to rip me wide open. For him, anger and sex were inextricably linked, and the angrier he was, the longer his attacks lasted. It meant nothing to him at all that I lay there sobbing and begging him to stop.

Then, one day, when Shuggie was thirteen (and I was sixteen), my father went into one of his rages and beat him so badly I really thought he had killed him. He had my poor wee brother's head between his knees, twisted so that Shuggie's face was looking up at him, and he was punching him so hard that Shuggie's head seemed to be swinging from side to side. I don't think Dad had ever beaten any of us quite as badly as that, and I was almost hysterical. I jumped up and down in front of him, punching and tugging at his arm and trying to pull Shuggie's head out from between his knees, screaming, 'Leave him alone. Please, please, Dad, stop!'

Shuggie's blood was spurting out all over the walls and, after a while, his face had swollen to about twice its normal size. Then, suddenly, he stopped struggling, and his body went completely limp. Giving him one final kick, my father's voice had a self-satisfied ring to it as he said, 'So, that'll teach you,' and then dropped Shuggie on the floor and walked away. What kind of monster could do that to his own child? Dad had a terrible rage within him, for reasons that had nothing to do with any of us, and I don't think he ever felt even the slightest twinge of remorse during all those years when we were kids and he vented his temper and aggression on us every day.

Thinking Shuggie was dead, I was sobbing as I rushed to the apparently lifeless heap on the floor. Crouching beside him, silently praying that he was still alive, I kept whispering his name and, eventually, he moved his head, very carefully and slowly. I almost fainted with relief – until I saw the state of him. Every single inch of his body was covered in bruises, and there was blood pouring from his nose, eyes and ears.

I reached out towards him, wanting to put my arms around him to try to comfort him, but there wasn't any part of his body that I could touch without hurting him. I couldn't bear to look at his poor, bloated face, so I just kept whispering over and over again, 'It'll be all right, darling. It'll be all right.' But it was as though I was really trying to convince myself because, in reality, I knew that Shuggie might well be going to die.

I tried to hide the terrible fear I was feeling, but the

tears were streaming down my face as I helped him into the bathroom and cleaned him up as best I could. He was sore all over, so all I could really do was help him get into bed. And that's where he stayed for the next few days, until he could walk again. It took two weeks for the bruises and cuts to heal enough for him to be able to go back to school.

Shuggie was quite a good boxer, and he never gave up on a fight, probably because none of his schoolboy opponents was ever going to be able to give him the sort of beatings he'd already had so many times at the hands of his own father. So Dad had a ready-made excuse, and blamed Shuggie's injuries on his boxing. But you could still see some of the bruises two weeks later, on Shuggie's first day back at school, and, that morning, one of my teachers told me he wanted to speak to me.

As I entered his room, the expression on his face was serious, and he looked directly into my eyes, holding my gaze as he said, 'Why has Hugh got bruises, Elizabeth? Is there something happening that you ought to tell me about?'

Suddenly, something seemed to snap inside me, and I was overwhelmed by an anger that was even more powerful than my usual feeling of guilt. I felt responsible for what had happened to Shuggie, and for what happened to both of my young brothers day after miserable day, and I hated myself every time I failed to protect them against my dad's ferocious attacks. At that moment, I had one clear thought in my head: 'I'm not going to cover for Dad any more. If I don't do something, he's going to kill one of us. He's evil, and I have to save the boys from him.'

With part of my mind, I was thinking about what Dad would do to Mum if I talked about what had really happened to Shuggie, and I had a sudden image of her lying broken and bruised and almost dead that day I came home without my wages. But although I loved my mum and wanted to protect her, Shuggie was just a wee boy who didn't deserve what had happened to him, and he had no one but me to fight for him. I knew I couldn't keep the secret inside me any longer and, bursting into tears, I let the words come tumbling out, telling the teacher about the beatings that had been part of our daily lives for as long as I could remember.

Once I started to talk, it was as though I couldn't stop, and I couldn't understand why I hadn't told anyone about it all before. But as I sat there, sobbing and telling the sorry story of our lives, I couldn't help thinking about what had happened last time I had told just a small part of my secret, and how my life had become even worse once Dad had been released from prison. The reality was that there was no way out. No one had helped us before, so why did I think things were going to be any different this time? Even so, it was a risk I knew I had to take, because I didn't think that any of us could survive much longer if something didn't happen to put an end to my dad's brutal attacks on us.

I couldn't talk about the sexual abuse, though. I had an enormous sense of guilt about it, because I still felt as though I was, at least partly, to blame for what Dad did to me. Even though, when he raped my body, it felt as though he was also raping my soul and infecting my whole being with his wickedness, there was a part of me that longed to be 'Daddy's special little girl' or 'Daddy's princess', which is what he sometimes called me as he pushed me down on the bed and ran his rough hands over my child's body. Although I realize now that it was just a child's longing for someone to love her, it felt at the time as though I was tainted by my father's lust, and I was deeply ashamed.

Above all, I knew that the sexual abuse was the main part of the secret that Dad had sworn me to keep, and that if I did talk about it, he was more than capable of carrying out his threat to kill my mum, without giving it so much as a second thought. I knew that although my main aim was to protect Shuggie and Alex, it was also my responsibility to try to keep Mum safe.

Later that morning, a social worker came to the school and took Shuggie and Alex to a children's home. I knew

I couldn't just disappear as well, because I had to get Mum out of the flat before Dad found out what had happened. So, as soon as the boys were safely out of the way, I went home, and while Dad was at the pub, Mum and I climbed out of a back window and ran and ran until we reached my gran's.

Gran's house was like a haven to me. As soon as you opened the front door, you could smell the wonderful aroma of soup and stovies wafting out from the kitchen, which was constantly full of people – my cousins and my mum's sisters. I used to sit in a corner and watch my aunts hugging and kissing their children, feeling stabs of jealousy as one of my cousins jumped on to my gran's lap for a cuddle. I longed to crawl into Gran's arms and tell her how much I was hurting, but I just couldn't bring myself to do it, because I felt that if I ever did let go enough to be able to give her a hug, I'd break. And, somehow, the thought of letting her cuddle me and surround me in her love without telling her my dark secret would have seemed as though I was being a traitor to her and abusing her trust. So I'd just sit in my corner, repeating over and over again in my head, 'I love you, Grannie,' and daydreaming about her hearing my silent screams or seeing the pain in my eyes and scooping me up into her arms to make everything better.

In fact, the only person I can remember ever giving me

a cuddle was one of my aunts, but as her arms went round me, my body went rigid, and I felt as though I was going to cry. I knew I could never lower my guard and run the risk of breaking down, so it turned out that the one thing I'd always longed for was something I couldn't take the chance and reach out for. I realized that day that, even if the opportunity were ever to arise again – which seemed unlikely – I could never allow myself to relax and be cuddled.

I'd become very good at putting up a front, and I think most people thought I was a monster of a child. I certainly had a chip on my shoulder and was fiercely protective of anything that belonged to me – which was actually precious little. If anyone touched something of mine, I could turn on them like a cornered animal. But I was nice to people if they were nice to me, and I look back now at the sorry wee wretch I used to be, and wish that somebody had just picked that child up and given her a good hug.

Mum and I stayed at Gran's for a while, then Mum went into a women's refuge and, after some time, into a house for the homeless, and I went to stay with my Uncle Jim and his girlfriend.

Uncle Jim had always been good to me, and I loved him. He'd caught me glue-sniffing a few months previously – I'd been hanging round with the wrong crowd and was happy to find any way of escaping from reality for a while – and he'd been really angry with me. He was no saint himself, but I was his little princess, and I think it made him realize that things must be pretty bad for me. He'd had to chase after me to catch me and, afterwards, he used to joke and say, 'You can run like a hare, you wee bastard. I've had to run from the police a few times, and I've never been caught. But I had to do a few laps to catch you, lady.' When he did catch up with me, I was out of my face, and he took me to my gran's house and just sat and held me until the effects of the glue wore off, and then took me home.

I wished later that I'd confided in my Uncle Jim, because I think that if he'd known more about what was going on, he could have made a tremendous difference in all our lives. He had a reputation for being a hard man, but he was always kind to me, and after he discovered some of what my dad was doing to me, he used to pop in regularly to make sure I was OK. There was at least one occasion when he found out that my dad had lifted his hand to my mum and he stepped in and sorted him out. So I think I was afraid that, if I told him everything, he'd kill my dad with his bare hands, and that was something I didn't want to have on my conscience.

Audrey was still living with our aunt, and Mary had gone to Italy. She came home one time, looking amazing and full of tales about how well she was doing out there, so my Uncle Jim bought me a plane ticket and I went out to Italy to live with her and make a fresh start.

The day I arrived in Italy, Mary took me straight back to the flat she was sharing with her boyfriend. We hadn't been there long when the phone started ringing. I smiled as she picked up the receiver and said, 'Pronto,' in a very impressive, Italian-sounding voice. But as she listened in silence to whoever was on the other end of the line, the colour slowly drained out of her face.

'I'm afraid you're going to have to repeat that, Gran,' she said, sinking into a chair and handing me the receiver.

'Hi, Gran,' I said anxiously. 'What is it? What's wrong?'

'It's your Uncle Jim,' Gran answered, in a shaky voice I'd never heard her use before. 'He's dead.'

I don't remember finishing the phone call or putting the receiver down. I collapsed into a chair, too, and that is where I sat for the next three hours, whimpering pathetically.

I couldn't believe Uncle Jim was dead, and I certainly couldn't believe that he'd taken an overdose. I often wondered if he'd got us all out of the way because he planned to make my dad pay for what he'd done to us – but I'll never know if that was the case, any more than I'll ever know what really killed him.

I got a job in Italy working on a television programme

called *Tutta la Casa*. I'd stand there holding whatever they were trying to sell while the guy who owned the shop said, 'This is what we've got in store today,' and then people would phone in and order things. Of course, I didn't speak Italian, so I never knew exactly what was going on but, apparently, one day, some man phoned up and said, 'If I come down to your shop, can I buy the lovely young girl who's holding the items? She's got the most beautiful smile I've ever seen.' I just went on standing there, not understanding what he was saying, which was just as well, because I felt very insecure about myself, and if I'd known what everyone was laughing and smiling about, my blushes would probably have heated the studio.

I had my first real kiss from my first ever boyfriend, a really nice boy called Luca, while I was in Italy, and it was the first time I'd ever slept with someone from choice. It was a revelation to me, because it wasn't 'having sex', it was 'making love', and it was completely different from what my father had been doing to me all those years. Luca was gentle and tender with me, and we were so happy together I felt as though I was living in a protective bubble.

After I'd been in Italy for only a few months, I had to go back home to appear in court for stealing a pair of shoes from Littlewoods before I left. I'd been sending money home regularly to my friend Jacky to look after until I got back, and as soon as my plane landed, I headed for her house to pick up my nest egg before going to see Mum. Although I knew that Mum had moved into a flat, I didn't have her new address and, as it turned out, Jacky didn't know it either.

'Don't worry,' she said. 'We'll just go up and ask your dad, and you can collect your money while we're there.'

For a few moments, my brain couldn't process what she'd said. I stared at her blankly, my hands damp with sweat and my heart starting to race.

'What do you mean?' I asked her, praying that I'd misunderstood. 'Why would I have to ask my dad for my money?'

'Well, because I've been giving it to him,' she answered, looking puzzled. 'Every time you've sent me some money, I've taken it up there – he's looking after it for you.' She paused for a moment, obviously worried by the expression she could see on my face, and then said, 'Why? What's the problem?'

Jacky and I had been friends for years, but although she knew some of the details of the life I'd lived at home, I'd never told her the full story, partly, I suppose, because I was terrified that, if she did know it all, she wouldn't want to be my friend any more. And now it looked as though the price I'd paid for keeping the secret was to lose all my hard-earned savings. But there was nothing I could do, except hope that by some miracle my dad might not have spent all my money on booze and that, perhaps, with

Jacky actually there in front of him, he might be persuaded to give it back to me. He was still living in the flat we all used to live in, so we went round to see him. I hadn't seen him since I'd told my teacher about his violent assault on Shuggie and I couldn't believe I had the courage to face him. I knew how much enjoyment he'd have got from using my money and from the thought that he was getting back at me. But would that be enough of a punishment as far as he was concerned?

You know how, if you long for something to be a certain way, you can sometimes convince yourself that it might be, despite all your knowledge and experience to the contrary? Well, going to my dad's house that night after being away in Italy, there was a part of me that clung to the hope that he'd have changed, that he'd be nice to me and say, 'I've been saving your money for you, Lizzie. Here it is.' It was stupid, of course, and, as I was to find out, a dangerous false hope. Dad was never going to change, and he didn't mind whose life he destroyed in his determination to dominate and control everyone who crossed his path.

Of course I didn't ever get my money back, but I did eventually find the address of the council flat where my mum was living, and I went to see her. She seemed pleased to see me, but I was completely shocked by the state she was in. It was obvious she was still drinking. There was no food – and precious little else – in the flat, and it wasn't long before I realized that I couldn't just turn my back on her and go back to Italy. I needed to come home and look after her, and perhaps I'd also be able to make a home for Shuggie and Alex so that they could come out of care.

I was really sad at the thought of not going back to Italy, but although Mum was still drinking, she was battling hard to overcome her alcoholism, and I knew I couldn't just walk away and leave her to fight it alone. So, ten days before my seventeenth birthday, Alex and Shuggie came out of care, and we all moved into Mum's flat, where I took charge of the household, determined to give my brothers some stability in their lives so that they could concentrate on their education and have the chance to make something of themselves.

Chapter Nine

Those few months I'd spent in Italy had given me a lot more confidence and I knew that, despite everything, I loved my mum and wanted to try to prop her up so that she could become the woman she should have been. And, over the next few months, we did occasionally see glimpses of who she really was, underneath the loud, often aggressive alcoholic who was only interested in where her next drink was coming from.

Dad was still living in the council flat where we all used to live, but, one night, just a few days after the boys and I had moved in with Mum, I was asleep in my bed when I thought I heard his voice. I had bad dreams every single night, so it just seemed to be part of my nightmare. But then I gradually began to realize that I actually *could* hear him, and as I struggled to wake up, I became aware that he was in my room, standing beside my bed and shaking me, saying, 'Wake up, Lizzie. I've just stabbed your ma.'

Confused and disorientated, I jumped out of bed, wrapping my arms around my body in an unconscious gesture of self-protection, and stumbled into the living room – and almost passed out at the sight that confronted me.

My mum was sitting slouched and motionless in a blood-soaked chair. Her face was ashen, and a horrible rasping sound was coming from deep within her throat with every shallow, painful breath she took.

Dad knelt on the floor beside the chair, saying over and over again, 'I'm sorry. I'm so sorry,' and at first I couldn't make any sense of what I was looking at. But then I noticed the knife on the floor beside where my father was kneeling, its blade thick with blood.

Alex had been woken up by the commotion, and I turned to find him standing beside me, his eyes wide with shock and with an expression of horror on his face that probably mirrored my own. It was obvious that Mum was dying, but for a moment my mind went blank and I couldn't think what to do. It felt as though my stomach was pumping acid up through my chest and into my throat. And then Alex and I shouted, almost in unison, 'We need an ambulance,' and Alex ran out to the phonebox, barefoot and shivering in his pyjamas.

As soon as he'd gone, blind panic overwhelmed me, and I ran out of the front door and stood on the landing shouting, 'Help! Help us! Someone help us, please!' My heart was pounding as I went from landing to living room and back again, feeling completely out of my depth and having absolutely no idea of what I should be doing. I was afraid to leave my mum alone with my dad, but I couldn't bear to listen to the dreadful sound of what I was certain were her dying breaths.

Eventually, after what seemed like hours, the ambulance and police arrived at almost the same moment, and Mum was lifted gently out of the chair – which by this time was so soaked in her blood you couldn't tell what colour it really was – and rushed to hospital. As they carried her out of the house, I stood in the hallway, shocked and sobbing, certain that I was never going to see her again.

By the time the police arrived, the knife that had been on the living-room floor had disappeared. After they'd taken Dad away, another police officer took statements from the boys and me, and then Alex went into the kitchen and stood at the sink, trying to make sense of what had happened, and overwhelmed by the thought that Mum might already be dead. He stood gazing sightlessly out of the kitchen window with tears pouring down his cheeks, and then turned away, wiping his face roughly on the sleeve of his pyjamas. Suddenly, his attention was caught by a dark stain that seemed to be seeping through from underneath the tray of eggs that always stood in a corner on the worktop. He reached out his hand and lifted the edge of the tray cautiously, revealing the bloodstained knife that Dad must have hidden there hurriedly before the police arrived.

Without touching it, Alex showed the knife to a police officer, and it was carefully removed and taken away as evidence. It was an important find, because it was a knife that Dad had brought from his own flat, which indicated that he'd set out that night with the clear intention of using it. He hadn't attacked Mum in a sudden fit of rage; his attempt to kill her had been a cold and calculated plan.

Although Mum and Dad were separated, and in the process of getting divorced, there still seemed to be a bond between them and, apparently, when Mum had answered a ring on the doorbell that night she hadn't been particularly surprised to find Dad standing there. She'd leant forward to accept his hug and, as she did so, he'd slapped her on the back. It was a rather harder slap than seemed necessary, but she thought nothing of it until she was walking ahead of Dad into the kitchen to make them both a cup of tea and he said, with a humourless laugh, 'I've just stabbed you, you know.'

At first, Mum didn't understand what he meant, and she tried to turn her head to look at her back, twisting her arm up behind her as she did so and feeling the handle of the knife that he'd embedded just below her shoulder. Shocked and starting to feel faint, she struggled to pull out the blade and, as she did so, she heard an audible hiss – the sound of her lung collapsing. At that moment, her legs gave way and she managed to stumble into the living room and sink into a chair, shock flooding her body as she tried to focus on Dad's face as he leant over her and almost spat out the words, 'If I'm not having you, then no one is.'

Mum wasn't expected to live. The knife had punctured her lung, and when we went to see her in hospital, she looked ghostly pale and fragile. She was hooked up to machinery to help her breathe and the expression in her eyes was one of exhausted defeat. However, although she was in hospital for weeks, by some miracle, she survived, and Dad narrowly escaped being charged with her murder.

The boys were taken back into care when Mum went into hospital, and they stayed there for the next three months before being allowed to come home again. Then, just before Christmas, I gave evidence at Dad's trial at the High Court. It was an ordeal I don't think I could have got through if it hadn't been for the support of my gran, who sat with me in the witness room holding my hand and hugging me and telling me that everything would be OK.

The proof against my dad seemed overwhelming but, amazingly, the case was found to be 'Not proven', and he received a verdict of 'Not guilty'. Goodness knows how this happened; it beggared belief. I tried to get hold of the transcript of the court hearing recently, but apparently it's been lost – there are hundreds and hundreds of detailed records of cases in the court's archives, but not that one.

Dad walked away from his trial a free man, proving yet again that *he* was in control. He didn't seem to be governed by the laws that govern the rest of us; he could do whatever he wanted to do and get away with it.

Out of hospital, Mum still wasn't having much success in her battle to come off the booze, and as she was spending almost every penny of her benefit money on alcohol, yet again it was down to me to make sure there was money to feed the family and take care of the bills, so I got a job at a large DIY store.

One of the guys I was working with was into 'buzzing' (glue-sniffing), and after I'd been there for about a year, the manager discovered that glue was going missing from the store. When this guy was questioned about it, he told them that I was the one taking it. I suppose blaming it on me was an easy option, because I *had* sniffed glue in the past, and I always looked completely worn out and was often late for work, because I had to walk there after I'd got Alex and Shuggie ready for school every morning.

But no one said anything to me at all until I went into work one morning and was told, 'Collect your stuff. You're fired.' They didn't have any proof, they were only going on what this guy had told them to save his own job, and although they believed that I was glue-sniffing, they didn't bother to ask me any questions to try to find out why.

I walked up the road sobbing. Without that job, I knew I couldn't go on putting food on the table for my brothers. It seemed that, however hard I tried, life was always going to be unfair. It was as if every time I took a step forward, an invisible fist knocked me down again, and I was tired of struggling to get on my feet and keep going.

For Mum, every day revolved around getting her booze and ciggies, and one day I was cooking our tea when she started asking me for money.

'I just need a few pennies for a drink, hen,' she said, over and over again until I thought I was going to scream.

'I keep telling you, Mum,' I snapped, for what seemed like the hundredth time, 'I don't have any money to give you. And if I did have any money, I'd have spent it on food so that I wouldn't be cooking one miserable Fray Bentos pie and trying to work out how to divide it up amongst all of us.'

All of a sudden, her wheedling changed to fury and she flung open the oven door with a crash, grabbed the pie and threw it out of the kitchen window. I stood there for a moment, stunned and unable to believe what she'd done, and then ran out into the garden, crying with tiredness and frustration, to see if there was anything I could salvage.

We ended up having nothing to eat that night, and I felt like I'd had the fight knocked out of me. The social workers allocated to Shuggie and Alex knew that I was the one looking after them and I just felt so weighed down by all the responsibility. But I knew if I showed any sign of vulnerability or inability to cope, the boys might be taken away and all my efforts would have been in vain. So I said nothing and no one offered to help.

Eventually, it all became too much to deal with and I moved out of Mum's flat and into a place with a couple of friends, got a bursary and started going to college to do a secretarial course. After a few months, however, Shuggie went to stay with Audrey, who had moved down to London, and Mum couldn't manage on her own and asked me to go back to live with her and Alex.

One morning, I woke up with a terrible pain in my tummy. I'd had a lot of really bad stomach aches as a child – the result of all my dad's punches and kicks – and this one was up there with the worst of them on the pain scale. Mum called 999 and I was rushed to hospital by ambulance, where I was told I needed emergency surgery to remove my appendix. I was still in agony when I woke up after the operation, and when the doctor came to see me, he said, 'It turned out that your appendix was fine. But we took it out as planned anyway, just as a precaution in case it should ever burst. However, we think the real problem might be with your bowel, so we'll have to look into that.'

In the meantime, I carried on at college – which is where I met Iain.

The first time I saw him, I remember thinking how beautiful his eyes were. I wasn't used to being 'struck dumb' by boys, but I got butterflies in my stomach before I'd even spoken to him. A couple of nights later, he was sitting in his car outside the place I used to work in the evenings, and he offered me a lift home. In fact, he didn't take me straight home, but instead drove to a car park that looked out over the lights of the town below, and we sat talking for hours, long into the night.

I couldn't believe how easy it was to talk to him and how natural it seemed to be just sitting there beside him in his car, gazing out over the twinkling lights. It felt as though I'd somehow come home.

After that, we spent almost every evening together, and, later, every night. Iain would go home to his mum's house after work, get washed and changed and have his tea, and then come to spend the night with me at Mum's flat.

One of the things I learned to love about him was that, although he could see the way we lived, and the state my mum sometimes got into, he never mentioned it. He seemed to know without having to be told that talking about it would be painful for me, so he didn't even try to discuss it. Even more importantly, he was good to Shuggie and Alex, and we'd often take them with us on our drives. They'd sit in the back of the car laughing and joking with

Iain, and I'd know that, for a while at least, they were safe and relaxed.

Then, one night when we were out together, I remember thinking, 'I've lived my whole life for other people. What have I really got to live for?' and I looked up at the sky and prayed silently, 'Please, God, give me someone who will love me just for me.'

I must have fallen pregnant within a week, although I didn't realize until about five months later that that was why I was being sick almost every morning. And when it did finally dawn on me, it was a huge surprise, because I'd been told I had severe endometriosis, as well as other gynaecological and bowel problems, and had thought that I'd never be able to have children.

Mum was still drinking, and I was still looking after Alex – and Shuggie when he was back from London – so I tried to struggle on for as long as I could. But I often felt really ill, and seemed to spend most of my time either sleeping or crying. There were days when I was frightened and didn't think I was going to be able to cope, especially as I hadn't really heard from Iain much since I had told him I was expecting. I was starting to think I might have to raise the baby alone. Then, one day, I was on my own in the flat when there was a ring on the doorbell, and I struggled up off my bed to the door and found Iain's brother standing there.

'Iain's down in the car,' he told me. 'He sent me up to see if you want to come to the cinema with us.'

Standing up had made me feel light-headed, and my skin was cold and clammy as I fought back yet another wave of nausea before answering him, in a voice weak with exhaustion.

'I can't,' I said miserably. 'I've been vomiting all day and I'm feeling really, really ill.'

'Oh, I'm sorry,' Iain's brother answered. 'Well, perhaps next time, when you're feeling more up to it.'

He turned around and left me standing there clutching the door for support, and it was another two days before I next saw Iain. I was tired of having to cope on my own. I'd hoped Iain would take my pregnancy in his stride, but it had obviously scared him more than I'd realized. After all, we hadn't been together for long and we were both very young. But it never crossed my mind to give up my baby; in fact, I was delighted that I finally seemed to be getting the chance for a new beginning.

Not long after that, I decided to finish things with Iain, not because I didn't want him in my life any more – in fact, far from it – but because it didn't seem fair to burden him with a child, as well as all the other responsibilities he'd be taking on if he was tied up with me. But a few days later, he came to my mum's flat and shouted through the letterbox, pleading with me to open the door and take him back.

'Please, Liz,' he called. 'Just open the door and talk to me. I know that you've been through enough already. But I'll never hurt you. I promise. I swear that I'll never let you down.'

It was as though, without having realized it, they were the words I'd wanted to hear. My prayer had been answered and I'd finally found someone who loved me for me. Someone who knew and understood the person I really was and who wanted to love and take care of me.

Sobbing, I threw open the door and hurled myself into Iain's arms, cupping his face in my hands and kissing him as we clung to each other. That night, we cried and talked for hours, until we finally fell asleep in each other's arms, knowing that, whatever else happened in our lives, we would always have our love for each other.

Towards the end of my pregnancy, I had to stop going to college, which meant losing my bursary. But on the day my daughter was born, I sat in the hospital holding her in my arms as she wrapped her tiny, perfect fingers around mine, and suddenly it seemed as though my life was complete. The love I felt for her was different from anything I'd experienced before, and I knew that things had changed for ever. Of all the responsibilities I'd ever had, protecting my daughter's precious new life was the most important one of all, and I was determined that I would never allow her to be hurt or let anything tarnish her perfection.

When I came out of hospital, Iain moved in to live with us in Mum's flat, and my life seemed to have turned a corner. Not only did I have a beautiful child, who I loved passionately from the moment I set eyes on her, but also, after all the years of having to cope alone, I finally had someone to help share the burden.

Iain was still just a teenager, and on a Youth Opportunity Programme, earning about £20 a week, but he helped to feed and support us all on his meagre wages, and he made me feel safe and secure. He was a good man, my Peter Perfect, and he became a rock in all our lives.

To me, sex was just sex, something that people did when they were married or in a relationship. As a child, I'd had plenty of opportunity to learn to detach myself mentally from what was going on around me, and that's what I did with Iain whenever we had sex. I'd switch off in my mind and imagine I was somewhere else, just like I used to do when I was a little girl, and, apart from the brief experience I'd had with Luca in Italy, it wasn't until years later that I was finally able to take part and connect emotionally.

In fact, I gradually became a bit of a prude, which must have been very difficult for Iain, although, at the time, I had no understanding of how he felt. He knew what I'd been through as a child, and I realize now how sensitive he was being, and how careful he always was to avoid asking me to do anything that might upset me.

Mum was still a hopeless alcoholic, but Iain was really good with her and used to tease her gently, and he was fab with my brothers. It amazed me that he didn't seem to begrudge spending his wages on supporting us all, and it felt wonderful to have someone to share my life with, someone who wanted to prop me up and help me, rather than needing my support.

Dad seemed to be doing all right too. He'd started a new building business and had a girlfriend and, one day, not long after my daughter was born, he brought this woman to meet us, because they'd decided to get married. She brought her adult children with her – one of whom had gone to school with me and my sister – and it was a really weird situation: having stabbed my mum and almost succeeded in killing her, Dad wanted to introduce her, and me, to his new wife-to-be. I just sat there, politely chatting to her as though it was the most normal situation in the world – which just shows how well conditioned I still was, and how I'd do almost anything to keep the peace.

At one point, Dad turned to me with a sneer and said, 'Do you know what the kids at school used to call you?'

I could feel my cheeks starting to burn, but I tried to ignore him, hoping that he'd let it drop rather than embarrass everyone in front of the woman he was, presumably, trying to impress. After waiting a few moments for an answer, however, he said in an even louder voice, 'I was just asking Lizzie if she knew what the kids at school used to call her – apparently it was "the fantasizer", because she used to talk about how she'd lived in an abusive household.' He gave a bark of humourless laughter and then paused, with a smugly satisfied expression on his face, before turning to his girlfriend and her daughter and saying, 'Isn't that right?'

Immediately, my heart started to race, and a cold sweat broke out all over my body. Desperate to head him off, and to stop anyone saying anything that might cause trouble, I quickly tried to change the subject. But I felt awful, like I was betraying myself, as well as the people who were going to take our place and become Dad's new family. It seemed as though Dad had won again.

Life went on. Iain was working, our daughter was growing into a lovely, confident little girl, and Mum seemed finally to be starting to win her battle against alcohol – most of the time, at least. Could I really be going to live the 'normal life' I'd always longed for?

Chapter Ten

After my daughter was born and Iain had moved in to live with us in Mum's flat, we were very happy. Shuggie was still in London, but Alex and Iain used to go out to work, and I'd clean the flat and cook their dinners for when they got home. I kept the flat spotlessly clean, because I was determined that no child of mine was going to live in the squalor that I'd had to live in and had always hated so much. Iain worked all hours, taking on extra jobs at the weekends so that we could save some money towards a deposit for our first flat. But we were really hard up.

Mum was still drinking heavily, and spending every penny of her benefits on booze. She wasn't a very dignified person when she was drunk. She used to go over the road to the pub, and often didn't make it back home afterwards, and I'd look out the window and see her lying in the street with her skirt up round her neck. So, I'd have to go down with my baby in my arms to pick her up off the ground and help her up the stairs. She'd also regularly wet herself and then just sit there screaming for someone to come and help her, and it would often be Iain who went in and sorted her out.

Mum didn't care about anything as long as she had a drink. But at least she'd stopped being aggressive, and although we bought all her food while she spent all her money on drink, it was her benefits that were paying the rent. So what could we say? It was *her* home, and we just had to put up with her demands, and buy her drink and ciggies when her money ran out.

There was a young single girl with a toddler who stayed across the way from Mum's flat and who worked really hard to try to better herself. One day, I was in the house, when I heard what sounded like glass smashing and, without thinking, I scooped my daughter up into my arms and walked out of the front door, just in time to see two big, burly guys climbing in this girl's window.

I could feel the anger rising up inside me, exactly like it used to do at school whenever I saw someone being bullied. Furious, and without giving any thought to how vulnerable I was, I shouted across at them, 'What the hell are you doing?'

One of the guys turned round and snarled at me, 'Get to fuck. Just get in yer house and keep yer mouth shut.'

'I'm sorry,' I thought. 'You've picked the wrong house there, friend.' Forgetting I was carrying my daughter,

I snapped back, 'No I bloody won't. She works hard for what she's got. You get away from that window.'

'And what do you think you're going to do?' he sneered. But then the thought must have crossed his mind that I wouldn't be being so brave if there wasn't someone to back me up, and suddenly he and his mate took to their heels and fled.

Later, when the girl came home from work and someone told her what had happened, she came over and knocked on my door, and said, 'Thanks so much for that, Liz. I wasnae insured, and I'd have lost everything if they'd got in.'

For me, stepping in had been an automatic reaction, because I hate the way some people pretend they can't see what's going on right underneath their noses. I'd suffered so much as a child from people choosing to look the other way and now I couldn't bear to stand there and not do anything. Those men were bullies, just like my dad – if he wanted something, he took it, with no care for what the consequences would be for anyone else – and people like that get away with it because no one wants to risk getting involved. I feel very strongly that it's everyone's responsibility not to ignore what's going on around them, and that we have to speak out about things that are wrong.

Iain and I tried and tried to get a place from the council, but without success. So we saved every single penny we could spare towards a deposit, and when my daughter was two, we bought our first flat. Even though it meant we had even less money than before, it felt like a fresh start, as though I was finally taking control and leaving my old life behind. We moved in with just a bed, a fridge and one beanbag, and for quite a long time all our meals came from the chip shop at the bottom of the road. But I knew that if we worked hard, we could make a lovely home for our little family, somewhere clean and happy that would be as different from the surroundings I grew up in as I could possibly make it.

Although we were always really short of money, I didn't go out to work until my daughter was four, because I was determined I wasn't going to leave her with anyone until she could talk well enough to be able to tell me if everything wasn't OK. Then I got a job in a computer factory, soldering components on to boards, and moved from there to another computer company, where I was doing twelve-hour shifts, trying to earn enough money to give my child all the things I'd never had when I was young.

I didn't work such long hours just because I wanted to earn the money – I needed to keep busy so I didn't have time to think, because, whenever my mind was free to wander, the memories and fears that came crowding in were too much for me to cope with. I was 'Lizzie Lipstick' – never seen without a carefully made-up face and a cheerful expression but, underneath the mask, I was the same, vulnerable, anxious child I'd always been.

When our daughter was five, Iain and I got married and, on the surface at least, my life was more than I'd ever dared hope it would be. But a couple of months later, something happened that was the first in a series of triggers that began to reveal the cracks that I'd so carefully papered over.

We'd gone out to buy some new tyres for our car, and as Iain was driving us home again, with the tyres stashed in the boot, he indicated and stopped in the middle of the road, waiting to turn right, across the traffic. Suddenly, there was a noise like an explosion, and a split-second later my daughter flew up into the air. I grabbed for her instinctively, and just managed to get hold of her before I started bouncing off every surface in the car. The last thing I remember is feeling a sharp pain running up my spine and into my head, and then I must have blacked out, because the next thing I knew, I was being cut out of the wreckage by the fire brigade. I was calling my daughter's name, and was frantic when I realized she wasn't in my arms. Later, I was told that when the impact occurred I'd grabbed her, wrapped my whole body around her and held her as tightly as I could, and they'd had to prise her out of my grip. Iain walked away from the accident with only minor cuts and bumps, and our daughter didn't have a single mark on her.

Apparently, the driver behind us had been yakking to her mum and had smashed into the back of us, sending our car bouncing across the road and up on to the kerb, and the back seats had been forced forwards into the front ones. I had been jammed in the tangled mess of metal, and spent the next few days in hospital. The paramedics who'd been the first to arrive on the scene of the crash came to visit me, and were astounded to find that I was recovering, because they'd been convinced I'd never be able to walk again. According to the police, it was our new tyres that saved us, by absorbing some of the impact of the crash.

I was lucky to have survived, but having to have time off work to recover meant that it was hard to keep my mind occupied and, a few months later, anxious and exhausted from lack of sleep I was referred to a psychologist by my GP. I was happy to talk to him about all my day-to-day, relatively trivial problems, but I never mentioned the real, underlying cause of my distress – my dad would have been proud if he'd known how well he'd conditioned me.

Then, a few months later, I fell pregnant again. It sometimes seemed as though I had a guardian angel watching over me, and every time life knocked me so low that I thought I couldn't pick myself up again, something happened to give me a reason to carry on. The thought that I might be able to give Iain the son he'd always longed for gave new purpose to my life.

However, our delight at the news was short-lived, and when I miscarried I knew that Iain was really disappointed – and I was devastated. I was sure that the gynaecological problems I'd always had were the direct result of what my father had done to me as a child, and so falling pregnant with our daughter had been a completely unexpected blessing. But now I'd been told that I wouldn't be able to have any more children, and it felt that the shadow my dad had cast over my life for so many years was going to taint it for ever. It was a devastating blow – the memories of abuse that I dealt with every day were already one life sentence, and now my father had helped hand me another one. He had robbed me of the chance to give my husband another child and my daughter of the chance to experience being a sister. My anger started to overwhelm me.

Everything became just too hard to deal with – I couldn't get dressed, the smallest things were such an effort . . . The next few months passed in a blur until, unable to find the strength to battle on any more, I took an overdose. But, as in everything, I failed, and my despair deepened at the thought that I couldn't even get that right, although, in reality, perhaps there was a part of me that didn't really want to die at all. Perhaps I was just exhausted from trying so hard to make a good life for us all, having to face one obstacle after another, with nothing ever working out the way I wanted it to. It was a cry for help, and I realized I couldn't let my anger and bitterness at what had happened to me ruin what I had.

By this time, Dad had built up his business to such a level that Alex, Shuggie and Iain were all working for him, Shuggie having moved back from London to take up the offer. So, for a while, Dad was back in our lives again. But then he bought a big house in the countryside and began to spend a lot of his time travelling and going on cruises, and it was while he was abroad one time that he had a major heart attack and had to be brought home by air ambulance. He survived, but his health remained poor for the next couple of years and, to my relief, we saw very little of him.

Then, one night, I was deep in a nightmare when I heard the shrill sound of a buzzer. It seemed to be part of my dream, but when it came again I slowly began to surface into consciousness and it became clear that the noise I was hearing was real. I lay in bed listening for a few moments, but I still couldn't work out what it was. I rolled over on to my back, feeling as though my head had only just hit the pillow, and tried to focus on the neon glow of the clock on the bedside table. One o'clock!

The buzzing sound came again, and finally I recognized

it as the front-door bell. Who the hell could it be at this time of night? I had to go to work in the morning, so whoever it was had better have a damn good excuse for waking me up. Iain muttered something incoherent and pulled the covers over his head as I swung my legs over the side of the bed, groped in the dark for my dressing gown and stumbled to the front door.

Still not firing on all cylinders, I opened the door a crack and was surprised to see my stepsister and her husband standing there, shuffling their feet nervously.

'Sorry, Liz,' my stepsister said, not looking directly into my face. 'Can we come in?'

Leading the way silently back up the stairs, I sat down on the edge of a chair, rubbing the sleep from my eyes and trying to suppress my irritation. What could possibly have possessed them to turn up in the middle of the night like this?

'You'd better get dressed, Liz,' my stepsister continued quietly. 'It's your father. He's in the hospital, and I'm afraid he's dying.'

Now it all made sense. Obviously, I was still asleep, and some evil part of my subconscious mind had conjured up a horrible wish-fulfilment dream. But, even after I'd pinched myself, I was still sitting in the living room in the middle of the night with my stepsister and her husband looking at me anxiously.

I went to the bedroom to wake Iain up, feeling stunned and completely numb and with a strange sensation of not knowing how to react, and a few seconds later he was struggling into his clothes and calmly taking charge, as he always did.

'I'll contact my brothers and sisters and we'll go to the hospital,' I told my stepsister, and as Iain led her and her husband to the front door, I could hear him saying, 'Thanks for coming out. It was good of you,' before adding, in a whisper, 'Don't worry, I'll see that she's all right.'

He was right: it *was* good of them to come out in the middle of the night rather than delivering the news by phone, which was how I was going to have to tell my brothers and sisters. Iain got our daughter up, while I made the phone calls to Mum, Alex and Shuggie. It was going to be a long drive to the hospital for us, but it was going to be a miserable and far longer journey for my poor sisters who were travelling from London.

Iain picked up everyone and we set off to the hospital. Mum and I sat in silence, lost in our own thoughts, while the others dozed on the back seat of the car. In reality, though, I wasn't really thinking at all, because my mind was a swirling mass of incomplete and disconnected images and I didn't seem to be able to concentrate long enough to make sense of anything. I felt completely emotionless, and again had the feeling of simply not knowing how to react, which was strangely uncomfortable, because surely anyone's reaction to the news that their father was dying should be automatic.

When we arrived at the hospital, we seemed to walk down miles of musty, damp corridors, which had a smell I can still remember clearly to this day. The atmosphere was claustrophobic; I felt as though the walls were closing in on me, and I had to force myself to keep going along the dimly lit passageways and not to turn and run back towards the large double entrance doors. None of us spoke, and the only sound was the faint echo of our footsteps on the worn, polished floors. Finally, we found the right ward, and I stood there, feeling disorientated and confused, while Iain went in search of a nurse.

The nurse opened a door to reveal my father lying in a cream-painted iron bed. The sight of him was shocking, and I hesitated in the doorway, unable to force myself to enter the room. He already looked like a corpse, but as though he'd been re-heated and re-vitalized just enough to be aware that we were there. His face seemed to have sunk inwards until it was almost unrecognizable, and his once-muscular body looked like a tiny, wasted rack of ribs, little more than a skeleton draped in loosely hanging, almost translucent skin. His chest didn't seem to be moving at all, but when I at last forced myself to step over the threshold and into the room, I held my hand just above his lips and could feel the faintest whisper of air, the only sign that he was actually still alive. Whatever I felt about my father, it was impossible not to feel pity for the person inside the helpless, wasted body that hardly made any visible outline under the bedcovers.

Leaving my mother at his bedside to say her farewells to the man she'd always remained a good friend to, despite their history together, the rest of us went in search of my stepmother and her children, who we found in the family room. While we were there, my oldest brother arrived with his wife, and they went in to see my father, who apparently had rallied enough to be asking for whisky and a cigarette. It would probably be the last thing he'd ever ask for, so although no one had any whisky, the nurses turned off the oxygen supply in his room and left him to have his final ciggie.

Waiting in the family room, I couldn't get rid of the shocking image of my father's frail, unmoving body lying in that hospital bed. Although he hadn't really been well since he'd been taken ill abroad and brought back home by air ambulance a couple of years earlier, we'd assumed it was just the aftermath of his heart attack. So it was a shock to all of us when we'd discovered he had cancer.

It was clear from the look of him that he might only have minutes to live, but somehow he was still hanging on when my sisters arrived after their long journey, and the three of us went in together to talk to the nurse.

'I'm sure you realize that your father is in a bad way,' she told us gently. 'He's slipping into a coma, and I'm afraid it's unlikely that he'll last till morning.' Then she left us for a few moments to allow the news to sink in.

All at once, the confusion and sense of unreality I'd had ever since I'd been woken up a few hours earlier disappeared, and I had a strange feeling of certainty about what I had to do.

I believe in God, and I believe that when we go to meet our maker, our hearts are weighed in the balance, and if you've been bad, you're going to suffer his wrath. So I know that my dad is going to be carrying his chains for eternity, but it doesn't make me feel sorry for him, because he deserves whatever punishment God gives him.

He'd hurt me too badly for too long for me to feel any real sympathy for him, or to feel any emotion towards him other than fear. But there was a part of me that couldn't let go of the thought that, despite it all, he was still my father. Even when I was a child and he was abusing me, both physically and mentally, until I often thought I was going to break into a million pieces, I'd sometimes long for some sign that, underneath all his cruelty and aggression, he loved me. I'd never completely abandoned the idea that there might be a bond between us.

But as I stood in that hospital room looking down at the shadow of a man my father had become, I felt numb. The truth was that any father/daughter bond that might have existed had long ago been destroyed, and the remnants of any love I once had for him were gone. But what I also realized was that it wasn't my job to judge whether he was good or bad. That wasn't my decision to make.

It was as though a fog had suddenly cleared in my mind, and I knew that I couldn't spend the rest of my life consumed by hatred. Dad would soon be judged – and punished – for all the terrible things he'd done in his life. But I didn't want to live the rest of my life dominated by resentment and still controlled by my father from his grave. I wondered how I'd feel in years to come if I let him die without doing what I could to ease his passing by telling him what I knew he wanted to hear. And I knew that I'd hate myself, and that I'd live to regret it if I didn't take this chance to try to set myself free from the hold he'd always had over me.

'I'm going to forgive him,' I told my sisters, surprising even myself with my lack of doubt and the firmness of my voice.

I went in search of the nurse, gave her a very brief outline of my story and told her what I wanted to do. It was obvious that she was shocked, but I could tell she approved of my plan and she agreed to help, returning to Dad's room with me and asking everyone else to leave.

I sat nervously on the chair next to Dad's bed. Terrified, and shaking uncontrollably, I was back in the world of my childhood again, feeling lost and uncertain and with nowhere to hide. However, I knew that this was something I had to do, for my own sake if nothing else, and gradually I managed to slow my breathing into a more regular pattern and calm myself down enough to be able to speak.

Then, while I was still struggling to find my voice, my father opened his bloodshot eyes and looked at me, and in that moment I felt sure that he knew why I was there. My body was rigid and my heart was thumping loudly against the inside of my ribcage and I gripped the sides of my chair so tightly my fingers ached as I fought back the urge to get up and run. Beads of sweat began to trickle from every pore, and my legs were trembling so violently that I had to clamp one hand firmly across my knees to stop my feet tapping noisily on the lino floor.

At last, I managed to gain some control over my body and, longing to be anywhere else in the world other than sitting beside the bed of my dying father, I said, in a hoarse whisper, 'I forgive you. I forgive you for what you did to me. I don't blame you. You can let go and go to heaven.'

Tears were streaming down my cheeks as, with one

final effort, I blurted out, 'I forgive you, Daddy,' and then broke down and sobbed.

A few moments later, when I raised my head again to look at my father, the slightest trace of a smile seemed to settle for a moment on his lips, and then he closed his eyes. Leaping to my feet, I flung the door wide open and shouted for the nurse, who ushered the rest of the family into the room.

Then, as everyone stood in silence around the bed, probably with very different thoughts going through their minds, my father seemed to try to say something. But the only sound that was heard was a quiet rasping noise as the last breath of air escaped from his body and he died.

Chapter Eleven

The drive home that day was one of the longest journeys of my life. For the last few years, I'd managed to lock away all the hurt, and had kept myself too busy to have time to think all the thoughts that crowded into my mind whenever I had a few minutes' peace and quiet. However, my father's death had now opened the floodgates. I felt as though I'd been punched in the stomach, and I sat silently in the car, my mind racing and my head starting to throb as the memories came flooding back. I'd fallen, face down, into a pool of despair and it felt as though someone had placed their foot firmly on my head to hold me there. All around me was a murky darkness that I simply didn't have the strength, or even the desire, to try to struggle out of. I didn't want to remember; I wanted to keep the pain at bay and force all the memories back into the box I'd locked them away in for so long.

By the time my father was buried, I still hadn't shed a single tear for him. When I sobbed at the hospital, it had been for my own pain, and for the memory of the frightened, pathetic little girl who'd suffered so badly at the hands of her own father. I know my father was a bad man, although I can't even begin to imagine what went on in his head. I will never forget what he did to me, and I'll bear the scars, both physical and emotional, for the rest of my life, but I am determined that I will not carry my father inside me.

Dad had a terrible temper, and it seems that he'd always been bad. I think he came from quite a strict background, but his brothers and sisters were all fine, so you can't blame whatever was wrong with him on that. There's a story the family used to tell about how he'd got into trouble with his dad when he was a boy for doing something that affected one of the neighbours in some way. In response, Dad went out at night and painted the neighbour's windows black, but not just the windows of that one neighbour's house – *all* the neighbours' windows. To me, the story just showed that he'd always had that sense of wanting to get back at people when anyone aggravated him.

Because Dad had become very wealthy by the time he died, a lawyer I talked to some time after his death suggested I should claim something from his estate. Just the thought of it made me shudder. I didn't want anything from him, because I knew that having some of his money would just make me feel dirty, as though he still owned a part of me.

The door that sealed off all my confused, frightening emotions had opened slightly when Dad died, but I slammed it shut again after his funeral, and my life continued more or less as normal. Every day, I kept myself busy with work, cleaning, cooking and looking after my family, right up to the moment when I collapsed into bed at night, and fell into an exhausted sleep. As long as I continued to lock away all the hurt and the memories in a dark corner of my mind, I could cope – or so I thought.

Not long after Dad died, Iain and I sold our flat and moved into a terraced house with a garden where our daughter could play. Mum went down to London to help my sister, Mary, when she had another baby, and stayed there for a couple of years. I thought that she was off the drink, although I found out later that she wasn't, and when she came back home and went to stay with her boyfriend, who was also a heavy drinker, she went back to getting drunk all the time. Mum was just a very weak person. She'd had a hard life, and it seemed to me that it was time for her to get a break. Eventually, she did manage to get off the drink altogether, and she started to become the woman she should have been. She'd still disappear to her boyfriend's for a bender for a couple of days from time to time, but when she wasn't drinking she was a completely different person, and she started coming round to the house and looking after my daughter so that I could go to work.

I can't remember Mum ever telling me she loved me, but I think she was trying to make up for some of her mistakes by helping out as much as she could, giving me a chance to have my life and to earn the money to give my daughter all the things I'd missed out on as a child. She'd often come into the room giggling and dancing; she just seemed to glow. My sister Mary's kids used to come up and stay for the summer holidays, and I'd get back from work and find Mum in the kitchen, humming cheerfully as she got the dinner ready, and all the kids running round the back garden. It was such a happy household, and she was fantastic when she stayed with us. As she grew as a woman, she started to take pride in her appearance and, one day when we were up in town together, I bought her a beautiful, green, pure wool jacket from House of Fraser. It cost £200, but she'd never had anything like it in her life before, and she looked great in it, and loved it. Finally, we were getting to know my real mum, the woman my dad had manipulated and almost destroyed, and although she wasn't strong, she was a really lovely person.

Over the next few years, we built such a good world for ourselves, with so many lovely people around us, that I felt we could cope with whatever life threw at us. That's not to say, though, that nothing bad happened during this period.

One day, when I was driving down the road with my daughter, there was suddenly a strong smell of fuel, but it disappeared when I slowed down and opened my window to find out where it was coming from.

'Something must have been spilt on the road,' I said to my daughter with a shrug, closing the window again and slowing to a halt at a crossroads. Then, as I glanced in the rear-view mirror, everything seemed to be moving in slow motion. The guy behind us jumped out of his car with a look of horror on his face. He seemed to be running towards us and was waving his arms, shouting something I couldn't hear, so I turned to open my window again and, as I did so, I saw flames licking up the side of my car.

I never swore at my daughter, and almost never raised my voice to her, so she nearly passed out with shock when I suddenly screamed, 'Get your seatbelt off. Now! Get your fucking seatbelt off.' But, as a surprise tactic, it worked, and I heard the click as she undid the buckle of her seatbelt.

The car had central locking, but it had already stopped working, and was making a wild whirring noise as it kept locking and unlocking the doors. The man who'd been in the car behind us was still trying to reach us through the flames, but by this time our car was filling up with smoke, and we were coughing and choking and finding it increasingly difficult to breathe. As I kept pushing frantically at the door, trying to open it, I heard a loud cracking noise and saw that the windscreen had begun to fracture in the heat.

At that moment, I was certain we were going to die, and I was crying as I threw the whole weight of my body against the door and tugged wildly at the handle. Suddenly, miraculously, the door flew open, and I managed to push my daughter out of the car before leaping out after her.

The man who'd been trying to help us grabbed me, and an old lady grabbed my daughter, and a few seconds after they'd pulled us away from the car, there was loud whooshing sound as it was completely engulfed in flames.

It was a very lucky escape – perhaps that guardian angel again – and the thought of how it might have ended still makes me go cold with fear when I think about it today.

Another horrible thing that happened during this period was that I was told I needed to have a hysterectomy. It was devastating news, for me and for Iain, and at that moment I hated my dad, because I was sure that it was what he'd done to me when I was a child that had permanently destroyed my chance of having another baby. I took time off work and went into hospital for the operation and, while I was recuperating, the enormity of what it all meant hit me like a bolt. Shortly afterwards, I took every pill I could lay my hands on.

Surprisingly, perhaps, I hadn't had any suicidal thoughts when I was young, mainly because I knew that I had to be there to look after my brothers, and that leaving them alone to fend for themselves simply wasn't an option. But after the hysterectomy I felt completely exhausted and emotionally drained. I just couldn't cope. I was too ill to do anything except lie on the couch all day and, with nothing to occupy my mind, I began to lose the battle I'm constantly fighting to block out all the memories and started to slip into a state of anxiety and self-loathing.

Even today, if I let my guard down for a moment, the memories that are always just beneath the surface force their way into my mind and, sometimes, however hard I search for something positive to cling on to, I'm swept away by depression and despair. I feel that it has always been my role to make people happy, so I thought I'd let Iain down, and I felt useless, as though I wasn't a real woman any more. Then a fear started to build up in my mind that my insides had had to be taken away because they'd been tainted by my dad and were dirty.

I loved my daughter more than I'd ever loved anyone in my life, and I was determined that I would always protect her and that no one would ever get the chance to hurt her. But as I lay on the couch day after day, the fears swirled round and round and stopped me being able to think rationally about anything. I didn't even consider what effect my death would have on my child – or on any of the other people who loved me. All I knew was that I couldn't take the strain of trying to hold everything together any more, and there didn't seem to be any other way out.

I survived my suicide attempt, and then hated myself even more when I realized how much damage I could have done to my daughter had I succeeded.

One night, just before Christmas, I was driving home after working the late shift when I heard on the radio that a young boy had been killed on the motorway when his car aquaplaned and crashed into a tree. I was distracted for a moment, feeling sad for the boy and thinking how horrible it would be for his family to be told such dreadful news, and I still hadn't shaken off the feeling of melancholy as I drove up to the house.

As soon as I'd stopped the car and turned off the engine, I knew that something was wrong. The Christmas-tree lights were still burning, which meant that Alex and Iain were still up, and I stood looking at the front of the house for a few moments, reluctant to go inside. I had a horrible feeling of dread that was making my stomach churn, but I took a deep breath, turned my key in the lock and opened the front door.

Iain stood up as I walked into the sitting room and,

wiping tears from his face with the back of his hand, said, 'You'd better sit down.'

'Why? What's happened?' I asked, still standing in the doorway of the room and looking from him to Alex and back again.

'It's Thomas,' Iain said at last. 'He's been killed in a car accident.'

I knew immediately that it was the accident I'd heard about on the radio, and I sank down on to a chair, put my head in my hands and sobbed.

Thomas and Iain had been very close for years, and Thomas had then become a good friend of mine, too, and had practically lived at our house. However, a few weeks previously, he and Iain had gone on a training course together, and when they got back, Thomas and I had rowed. Looking back, it was a silly argument, but we'd both over-reacted, and although he still came to the house as usual, we'd stopped being quite so close. Thomas was a lovely, caring boy, and I'd always known that we'd eventually sort things out and be close again. But, now, we never would. Now, he was dead and, as well as being heartbroken, I felt deeply guilty for not making things right with him when I had the chance.

The following year, we sold our house and moved a couple of streets away. We hadn't been planning to move, because we'd worked so hard on getting everything in the house just the way we wanted it. But when Iain changed jobs, he started having to park his van outside, and several of the neighbours complained. So we found a larger house with a garage – and finally I stopped imagining that I could hear Thomas calling out to me in the garden as he came through the house after work in the evenings.

The new house was like something out of a time warp, but we knew that we could transform it with a bit of hard work and, importantly, it had a bedroom for my mum. To get it at a good price, we needed to act fast, so we took out a bridging loan and bought it before we'd sold our old house. It was an unusual thing to do at the time, but I knew that if I wanted good things to happen in my life, I had to be bold and take risks. We worked out our finances, gave ourselves three months to sell our original house, packed up our stuff and moved into the new one with Mum, and then set about ripping everything out and re-doing it all.

As time ticked by and there was still no sign of a buyer, Iain used to pace around the living room, waving his arms in the air and shouting, 'Oh my God! We've not sold the house. Tell you what, I'll throw in the mother-in-law for nothing. She's very good at cleaning!' He was very good with her, and was always winding her up and making her laugh. Thankfully though, the house did sell, and life resumed its normal path.

Mum had had a tough life and, the older she got, the more I wanted to look after and protect her. In one of the social work reports that was written when we were children, one social worker states that he thought she may have been more manipulative than she appeared, but I don't believe that. She was a sad, pitiful, hopeless alcoholic who was living with a man who was much stronger than she was and who beat her so many times that she lost the ability, and the will, to fight back.

I never questioned her about the past, and didn't blame her for allowing all the things that happened to me when I was young. I felt that we had to enjoy the present and concentrate on getting back to being a family, and I thought I had the perfect family household. This was a happy time for me, and I had a tremendous sense of satisfaction watching my mum laugh and relax, knowing that I was letting her grow and be herself. As far as I was concerned, it was time to bury the past.

If sheer effort could heal emotional and physical scars, I'd be living a very different life today. But the reality is that however many times I tell myself to forget the past and concentrate on the future, there are some things I know I'll never completely come to terms with. And one of them is the effect my father's treatment of me as a child has had on my health.

A few months after I'd had the hysterectomy, I was back

in hospital again for surgery to remove my large intestine. I'd always suffered from stomach aches, and they'd continued after I'd had my appendix removed, unnecessarily, as it turned out. It finally got so bad that I couldn't go to the toilet – I was given some tablets to swallow and a week later they were still in my tummy – and that's when they decided they needed to do something quickly. I was really frightened by the prospect of having bowel surgery, but there was also a part of me that welcomed the thought that at least it might put an end to all the problems I'd been having for so long.

Thankfully, the operation went well, and although I was once again stuck at home recovering, with all my thoughts swirling around my mind, I was just about coping – until the wound became infected and I had to go back to hospital to have an abscess removed and all the infection cut out. After that, they couldn't stitch me back up again, and I ended up with a foul-smelling hole in my tummy that was big enough to put your fist into.

I was in terrible pain, and I couldn't do anything without someone there to help me. Iain used to get me down the stairs to the couch in the mornings before he went to work, and then I'd be stuck there, unable to move, or even roll over, because I couldn't use my stomach muscles. A nurse came every day to clean the wound and help me into the toilet. Then she'd put me back on the couch again, and that's where I would stay till Iain came home from work and made the tea. I lived like that for weeks, just lying on the couch, frustrated and depressed, my head buzzing with memories, until at last I was able to go back to work and start trying to get my life into some sort of order again. It was a frustrating time, especially as I had a new house to organize and we really needed me to be working so we could pay off the loan we had taken out.

The year that I had my bowel surgery, Mum was in and out of hospital too. She'd stopped drinking by then, but she had problems with her stomach, and her pancreas was shot to pieces because of the booze. The doctors ran all sorts of tests, but they couldn't find out what was wrong with her.

After we moved to the new house, Mum had her own room with her own TV, and she seemed to be happier than I'd ever seen her. However, although she was living with us, she'd often stay at her boyfriend's house, and one night when she was there she had such terrible pain in her back that they called out the doctor.

When I saw her the next day, she seemed really miserable. She told me that the doctor had said she had to lie on a hard floor for twenty-three hours every day.

'Indeed you will not,' I answered. 'You'll come up and stay with us, where you can lie in your bed and watch your telly.'

She agreed to come home and it was obvious that she was trying her best to be cheerful.

Over the last few years, we'd got into the habit of going out shopping together, and we were up in town one day when she suddenly said, 'I need to sit down, sweetheart. I'm awful tired.'

We found a bench to sit on and I said, jokingly, 'You'll be all right. You're just getting old.'

'Aye, I think that's what it is,' she answered with a smile. 'I think old age is catching up with me.'

My heart gave a lurch and I had a horrible, inexplicable feeling of panic, but I kept up my teasing tone, saying, 'Don't give me any of that, lady. You get up and get on with it. Come on!'

We went into another shop, but I was seriously worried about how tired she looked, and after a while I took her home.

That night, she went to my older brother's for her dinner and then to see her boyfriend. But, again, they had to phone the doctor, and she was taken into hospital for more tests. They found a lump in her chest and took a biopsy, but by the time the results came back she was already really ill. She was started on chemotherapy, but she wasn't strong enough to take it, and when she had a body scan, they found that the cancer was everywhere – and that it had started in her lung, the lung that Dad had stabbed.

Alex, Hugh and I took it in turns to stay with Mum at the hospital as much as we could. The doctors put a suction tube down her throat to drain her lungs, but we used to roll her on to her side regularly to help get rid of all the fluid that built up, and we'd sit talking to her and doing whatever we could to try to make her more comfortable.

One night when I was at the hospital with a friend and some of my aunts, Mum sat up in bed wearing her satin jammies and a pair of sparkly earrings I'd bought for her earlier that day, and sang 'Hey, Big Spender'. She was a fantastic singer, and I really felt for a moment that the doctors might be wrong and that she might fight back and beat the cancer after all.

Then, while everyone was still laughing and congratulating her on her fine singing voice, she turned to me and said, 'I need to speak to you alone, Lizzie. Can you come back later, when you've been up the road? There's something I need to tell you.'

I knew that my aunts wouldn't leave until I left, so I waited a few minutes and then said, 'We all need to go now so that Mum can have some rest,' and I went home with my friend.

Later that evening, when I was ironing some clothes to take to the hospital for Mum, I was suddenly overwhelmed by a feeling of panic. Switching the iron off, I said to my friend, 'I need to go back up there.'

My friend came with me to the hospital, and as soon as we went into Mum's room, Mum whispered in a frightened little voice, 'The spooks are in here.'

'What do you mean, Mum?' I asked her, feeling completely freaked out.

'There's trouble between my mum and dad,' she answered.

'But your mum and dad are dead,' I said gently.

'I'm going to get into trouble,' she murmured, as though she hadn't heard me. 'I cannae tell you any more. I have to go now. They're listening to me, and I'm going to get into trouble.'

She looked frightened, and I could feel the hairs on the back of my neck stand up and my skin turn cold and clammy.

'Who's Scott?' she asked suddenly, her voice stronger and no longer whispering.

'I don't know, Mum,' I answered. 'I don't know anyone called Scott. I don't know who you're talking about.'

'You will one day,' she said, squeezing my hand lightly. 'You're going to go through a hard time, but you're going to have a wonderful life. I cannae tell you any more. I'm sorry, darling, but I'm so tired.'

'It's all right,' I told her. 'Don't worry, Mum. Just sleep. I'll come back later with your jammies.'

But by the time I got back with her clean, freshly ironed pyjamas, she'd slipped into a coma.

'I'm afraid she won't be coming out of it again,' the nurse told me.

However, I was determined that she wasn't going to die. In any case, I'd promised her that when the time did come, she'd die at home with me, not in a hospital bed, surrounded by tubes and machinery. 'She will come out of it,' I snapped back at the nurse. 'I know she will. I want to take her home.'

'She'll be lucky if she lasts the weekend,' the nurse answered bluntly.

'No, you're wrong,' I almost shouted at her. 'She *will* last the weekend.'

In fact, she died, in hospital, the next day, leaving the children and grandchildren who loved her so much completely heartbroken. It wasn't until years later, when I looked back on that night and saw her wee face trying to reassure me, that I asked myself how she knew what the future held in store for me.

Chapter Twelve

After Mum died, every single penny she'd saved went on her funeral. Three pipers played outside the church, which was decorated with masses of huge white lilies, her favourite flowers, and she was buried wearing the prettiest dress and in the best coffin I could buy.

I still have the green woollen jacket and a cameo brooch I bought her, which she wore with everything, and I carry her bus pass in my purse. I still miss her, every day of my life.

Hugh and Alex were devastated by Mum's death, too. They'd been moving backwards and forwards between Mary's house and mine and, although Alex had gone through a phase of getting into mischief, he was working really hard by that time, and meeting some really nice girls. Shuggie had also been successful at work, and had become the manager of a big supermarket near London, and was so lovable and good-looking that all the girls were falling at his feet. I was really proud of them both.

Then, while I was working at the computer company, Shuggie came back to live with us. He'd started talking to himself and acting a bit strangely even before Mum died but, to begin with, I just thought he was being silly. It got to the stage, though, when I'd get home from doing a twelve-hour shift at work and find him wandering around the garden singing to himself and having whispered conversations in empty rooms. He seemed to be drifting away from reality, and I began to get really frightened for him. The situation was starting to take its toll on my health too, and I knew we couldn't go on like that.

Then, one day, I saw him walking down the road with his headphones on, hitting himself in the head and singing out loud. People were laughing openly at him, and I realized that I had to do something to help him. So I took him to see my doctor, and she gave me a letter and told me to take him up to the local psychiatric hospital for an assessment.

I knew that Shuggie wouldn't agree to come with me if he knew what was happening, so I lied to him and told him that I had to see a doctor there and that I didn't want to go on my own – and he came with me, like a lamb to the slaughter.

When we arrived at the hospital, I handed the doctor's letter to the nurse in charge and she nodded towards a row of seats, saying, 'Just take a seat and someone will see you soon. It won't be long.'

However, we waited for what seemed like an eternity,

and Shuggie was starting to get agitated and ask questions. I've never been the most convincing liar in the world, and I knew that my answers were becoming increasingly pathetic. Then, suddenly, he stood up and started edging his way towards the door, looking around suspiciously. Just at that moment, two large men appeared and grabbed him by the arms. Shuggie began to scream and try to fight them off, and I nearly jumped out of my skin with fright. But these two blokes – who looked like bouncers at the door of a club – held him down while someone gave him an injection, and finally he stopped struggling and they took him off to a ward.

I stood there feeling cruel and helpless, crying and saying, 'I'm sorry, Shuggie. I'm sorry.' But I don't think he even heard me.

He was kept, heavily sedated, in a locked ward at the hospital for the next few days and then diagnosed as having schizophrenia. I went to visit him the day after he was sectioned, and I'll never get the memory of it out of my mind – the smell of the hospital and the look of shocked disbelief and hurt confusion on his face as he asked me, 'What have you done to me?'

I was completely swamped by guilt and shame and by the terrible feeling that he'd trusted me and I'd betrayed him. When I left him at the hospital that day, I sobbed and sobbed until I thought my heart would break, and clung desperately to the thought that the ends justified the means. However difficult it was for me, I had to do what was best for Shuggie and try to get him the help he so obviously needed. Later, he did seem to understand that, because he told me one day, when he was on medication and living a more normal life again, that although he'd been angry with me to begin with, he was grateful for what I'd done, because he knew that, without treatment, his life wouldn't have been worth living. I knew in my heart of hearts that he was right, but I don't think I've ever really forgiven myself for lying to him and tricking him like that.

It's possible that the stress of what had happened to Shuggie played a part in making my bowel problems even worse, because, working the night shift about a month later, I started having the worst stomach pains I've ever had. I wanted to stay at work, so I tried to carry on, stopping every so often and sitting with my knees pressed up against my chest, and going backwards and forwards to the company's medical office to take Gaviscon. Eventually, my boss complained that I was spending too much time away from my station, but the nurse was worried about me, so she phoned Iain and told him to come and collect me and take me up to the hospital. A few hours later, I was having emergency surgery to untwist my bowel, which had formed into a loop and gone into spasm and was slowly strangling itself.

Unfortunately, although I take tablets every day, nothing can really be done to cure the problem. It still happens from time to time, and all I can do is make sure I get to hospital quickly when the pain starts. The last time was really bad, and the doctors came very close to removing the rest of my intestine and giving me a colostomy bag, although in the end they decided to wait a few days to see if it would untwist itself again, which, fortunately, it did. It's only really a matter of time, though; it's something I'm just going to have to accept.

Four months after my operation, I was woken up one night by the sound of the telephone ringing. Still groggy with sleep, and with my eyes firmly shut, I reached out my hand and groped around on the bedside table. When I picked up the receiver, I could hear someone sobbing on the other end of the line. It took me a few seconds to realize that it was Shuggie's girlfriend. She was crying so much I could hardly understand what she was saying, although eventually I managed to make out the words: 'Shuggie's dead.'

I could feel hysteria rising up inside me, and I grabbed Iain's arm and started shaking it and shouting, 'Iain, wake up! Get your clothes on. Move! It's Shuggie's girlfriend. She says he's dead. We're going up there.'

By the time we arrived at Shuggie's flat, the paramedics were already there and the whole place was swarming with police. As I pushed my way through the front door, an arm reached across in front of me and a man's voice said, 'You cannae go in there.'

'What do you mean, I cannae go in there?' I shouted, dodging under his arm and pushing my way towards the living room. 'That's my wee brother in there, and no one's stopping me from getting in.'

Shuggie was lying on the couch in his boxer shorts, looking perfectly normal, and I almost laughed with relief. He was fine, as I'd known he would be. It was all some sort of sick joke – it simply wasn't possible that anything could have happened to him. I knelt by the couch and touched the icy-cold skin of his arm, and it was then that I realized he had already gone.

All my life I'd fought so hard to make sure he and Alex survived; to push them out of harm's way whenever I could, even if that meant taking some of the beatings my father had intended for them. Before my daughter was born, my young brothers were the only reason I had for living, because I knew they needed me. For years, my sole purpose in life had been to take care of them – and then I'd turned my back, just for a few moments, and Shuggie was dead. At just twenty-seven years old, he'd choked on his own vomit and died. How had I allowed that to happen? It was my responsibility to protect him, and I'd failed in that one, simple duty and let him die. I became convinced that, if I hadn't taken him to the doctor that day and then tricked him into hospital, he'd still be alive. So, in fact, not only had I failed to protect him, I'd actually killed him – and I continued to believe that for a long time.

It was the final blow. In the space of just three years, I'd lost my chance of having another child, I'd had half my intestines cut out, I'd lost my mum, and now I'd lost my brother. My world was falling apart around me, and no one could offer me any comfort.

After Shuggie's death, I finally broke; I simply couldn't take any more. I'd spent my whole life fighting – fighting to try to protect myself and my young brothers when we were children and to make sure we all survived, and fighting against the depression and anxiety that threatened so many times to drag me under – but now it felt as though I'd lost the battle once and for all. All the stuffing seemed to have been knocked out of me and I was ready to curl up into a ball and give in. The bottom had fallen out of my world and I wanted to push anyone who loved me, or anyone I loved, out of my life, because loving people was too painful. The only person I needed was my daughter. If we clung together, no one could hurt us.

Chapter Thirteen

After I lost my mum, I was referred to a psychiatrist, who treated me for a few months for severe depression and anxiety. Although I always had a feeling of anxiety just below the surface, if I kept busy, I could often block it out for quite long periods at a time. But then something would happen that would act like a trigger, and I'd be plunged back into depression again. It had been really bad after my daughter was born, partly because I suddenly had the huge responsibility of having to protect her against all the terrible things I knew existed in the world. I'd taken anti-depressants for a while then, too, and had eventually managed to cope again – at least, enough to function fairly normally. But when Shuggie died I was devastated; his death knocked me off my feet completely, and I just couldn't see how I was ever going to get up again.

My world just seemed to have crumbled, and one day I looked inside myself and thought, 'What have you ever done for yourself? Your life has always revolved around Alex and Shuggie, and now one of them is lying dead.' That night, I sat in bed looking at Iain as he lay beside me and I knew that I was living a farce. It felt as though I was living my life just to keep everybody else happy. Didn't I deserve to be happy too?

A few days later, I was busy in the kitchen when my daughter came in and asked, 'Is dad due home from work soon?'

'Oh, aye,' I answered, without looking up from the pan I was stirring. 'He'll be home soon.'

'Oh,' she answered listlessly, giving an almost imperceptible shrug.

Surprised by the sadness I could hear in her voice, I stopped what I was doing for a moment and turned to look at her. Seeing the expression on her face, I realized with a jolt that I was as miserable as she looked. The atmosphere in the house had been heavy for months and it became clear to me that my heart wasn't in the marriage any more.

I knew that Iain loved us both. He often used to cuddle us and tell us so. But he never seemed to have any time to spend with us, and suddenly I knew I had to face the fact that we'd grown apart.

There was no denying that Iain was a rock to us. He'd stood by me and supported me for fourteen years, and I'd never been able to believe how lucky I'd been to find him. Whatever else happened between us, I knew that I'd always be grateful to him for giving me my daughter, because if

I hadn't had her, I'm pretty sure I wouldn't be alive today. But my world had been turned completely upside-down by the devastating loss of my mother and then Shuggie, and although I didn't realize at the time quite how badly I'd been affected, something inside me was making me push away anything good in my life. To shut out the nightmares that haunted me, both sleeping and waking, and to stop my mind endlessly going over and over all the memories that were always threatening to engulf me, I was working long hours and was completely exhausted. I wasn't creating the happy household I wanted, and I knew I had to make a change. I was miserable. I wanted the best for my daughter, and I knew that 'the best' included a happy home life.

It seemed as though I was failing her, tainting her life with my own misery. I didn't feel I deserved to be loved, and suddenly the solution seemed obvious. When Iain came home that evening, I said simply, 'It's over.'

It was as though someone else was speaking in my voice, and I don't think I really had any idea what I was doing. Life seemed to keep knocking me down, and I'd got to the point when I didn't think I'd ever be able to get back on my feet again. I started shutting everyone out because if there was no one left in my life, I wouldn't have to go through the pain of losing anyone ever again. What I didn't realize, though, was that I was pushing out all the good things, and hurting the people I loved. I was intent on hitting the self-destruct button, and there was nothing anyone could do to stop me.

After Iain and I split up, I was in a complete daze, just looking after my daughter and going through the motions of leading a normal life. But all the time there was a pain deep inside me that would sometimes hit me with such force that it almost knocked the breath out of me, and I'd lock myself in my room and sob until I had no tears left to cry.

I think Iain thought I'd been seeing someone else while we were still together, but I didn't even kiss another guy until after we separated and I started seeing Peter. Peter was a really lovely guy, and I believe that if things had gone differently, we'd be married now. However, every time he stayed overnight, Iain would turn up and stand outside the house shouting. I didn't think about it at the time, but it must have been difficult for Iain knowing that another man was with his wife and daughter in what used to be our family home. He was really upset and his mates hated seeing him in such a state, so they took it upon themselves to do something about it. It all came to a head when some guy Iain and I both knew turned up on my doorstep when Peter was with me and told me, 'Get him out of there. If your mother could see you now, she'd turn in her grave.'

I was furious, and sick of being controlled and manipulated, so I shouted back, 'It's got fuck all to do with you. Don't you ever judge my life! Take a good look at your own, and then you about-turn and get off my doorstep.'

However, shortly after that I realized that I was going to have to finish with Peter, to protect both him and my daughter. I was devastated, because I really loved him, and I know he loved me, but all my conditioning as a child made me afraid of what might happen if things got out of control and I ended up endangering him. Without giving him any explanation, I stopped seeing him, and then, one day, the doorbell rang, and when I opened the door Peter was standing there.

'I can't talk to you now,' I said, biting my lip to hold back the tears and starting to close the door again.

Peter held out his hand as if to stop me, saying, 'Wait, Liz. Please. I don't understand why you're finishing with me. What happened? Tell me. Please.'

'I can't tell you. I just can't,' I cried, the sight of him standing there looking hurt and bemused imprinted on my mind as I banged the door shut.

I was heartbroken, and I felt really guilty, because he's a lovely guy, and he didn't deserve to be dumped like that – apparently out of the blue, without any explanation. For the next few nights, I sat on my own in the living room after my daughter had gone to bed and cried bitter, resentful tears at the thought of what I'd lost. And it was on one of those nights, when I was feeling lonely and vulnerable, that a guy I knew vaguely called Frankie turned up on my doorstep, invited himself in and tried to comfort me, reassuring me that I'd done the right thing by putting an end to my relationship with Peter.

Frankie was quite short, had white-blond hair and a slight limp and seemed like a really nice guy. I was grateful for the company and for someone to talk to, and we started seeing each other. I had put the house on the market, and when it sold and I moved into a flat, he was waiting in the wings.

I was moving all my furniture bit by bit, in the car, because I didn't have any idea how to go about getting a van, when Frankie offered to help. It was a fateful decision to trust him, for a lot of reasons, but I was so desperate to be loved that I completely missed – or ignored – any of the signs. It started off as a casual arrangement, but after a while we were seeing each other a couple of times a week.

One night, I was at a party, sitting beside a girl I knew slightly, who was chatting away to me and playing with my hair, when she suddenly said, 'What would you do if you were involved with a guy who was in another relationship, but he didnae really want to be in that relationship? He was forced into it and he wasnae happy. What would you do?'

'I'd tell the girl that he didnae want to be with her, and then I'd take myself out of the situation until he wasnae involved any more, and then I'd see him,' I answered innocently.

'Oh, right,' she said in a thoughtful voice, twisting the ends of my hair gently around her finger.

And that was that. I didn't think anything more about it, and I didn't have a clue that the girl she was talking about – who was proving to be such an inconvenience in her own love life – was me.

Frankie spent a lot of time drinking down at the local bar, where he got on well with the owner, doing a bit of work for him now and again. After we'd been together for a while he asked if I'd like to help him out with some PR work and I started going round with a bunch of young girls in a van at night before the bar opened. We'd give out flyers at all the local pubs and clubs, which meant I was spending a lot of time at the bar at odd hours. Then, one afternoon, I was having a drink with Frankie and some of the other guys, sitting in a dingy alcove, when someone put some white powder in front of me and said, 'Try this.' I wasn't gullible – I knew that it was cocaine – and I was very anti drugs. Being slightly asthmatic, and someone who only needs a couple of drinks to make her merry, I was worried about what effect drugs might have on me, and I had always been too terrified to try them. I was convinced that just one ecstasy pill, for example, could kill me, so taking coke was completely out of character for me.

But when someone wants you to join in with them, they don't give up till they've worn you down, and Frankie kept saying, 'Go on. Try it. Just try one line. You'll love it.' So, after resisting for quite a while, I did – and, before I knew it, I'd developed a coke habit that ended up costing me everything I had. I started off paying for my coke and for Frankie's from the money I was earning at the bar, and I ended up cashing in my endowment policies and spending every single penny of my savings. I must have seemed like all Frankie's Christmas presents rolled into one.

Even after I'd spent all I had, he still went on demanding money from me, and then started beating me up when I couldn't get any for him. I was so desperately anxious for life to be perfect that I looked at everything through rose-tinted spectacles, and didn't notice what was going on right underneath my nose. However much I might have fought against it, doing what I was told had been ingrained in me from a very early age. So, for someone like Frankie, I must have been laughably easy to manipulate, because all I really wanted was to love and be loved and to avoid any sort of conflict. But perhaps the main reason I got hooked on coke was because there were more demons living in my mind than most people could even imagine and, for the first time in my life, I'd found something that could knock them out for a while and let me rest.

It was as if taking coke wasn't illegal. We'd take it everywhere and anywhere, and even put out lines on a table in the bar. It got to the stage when I was using an ounce a day, and I began to pitch in with friends to buy it in large quantities, as it was cheaper to get it in bulk.

There were a bunch of regulars at the bar who terrified everyone – the kind who wouldn't move out of the way to let new customers in to order their drinks without a shove and a glare, a menacing lot who enjoyed their power. I'd grown up with worse, though – what with my dad having been involved in various types of criminal activity, including threatening and hurting other people – so I didn't really think too much of it, until one night I finally realized what I was in amongst and that I couldn't carry on living like that. I had to get myself off the drugs, for my daughter's sake more than anything. A drug habit makes you selfish, and I realized that I was endangering my relationship with her by putting my addiction first.

The moment I stopped and reflected on what my life had become, it was clear to me that I'd sunk to an all-time low, and I sat and cried when I thought of all the misery I must be causing. I knew I had to make a fresh start for us both, and that I had to get myself out of the life I was living before it was too late – because, if I carried on the way I was going, the future looked bleak.

When I looked back on the traumatic experiences I'd lived through as a child and to how I'd managed to drag myself up from having nothing to having what Iain and I had when we were together, I knew that I had the strength somewhere within me to turn things around and give my daughter the future she deserved.

Deep down, I knew that my relationship with Frankie was over and that I was just kidding myself, going through the motions. I had to break the pattern of seeing him. The flat my daughter and I had moved into after my split with Iain was in a bad area, and she'd started hanging around with some dubious characters. I wanted her away from there, and that is what finally gave me the courage to cut all my ties and move into a privately let flat. It wasn't a million miles away from where we'd lived before and by this time I was struggling with money, what with paying the new rent and also dealing with my drug debts. But Frankie would still come round and ask me over and over again to give him money to buy coke, and then fly into a rage if I refused, or if I simply didn't have any money to give him. I knew I was on a path to self-destruction, which is why I started trying to come off the drugs, and so, apparently, did Frankie. We were in an absolute mess.

One night, I was staying in his flat with him when he started punching me. Instantly, I was a child again, bruised and scared and cowering in a corner trying to protect my head. Then, as though a switch had been flipped in my brain, my fear turned abruptly to anger. This wasn't my father; I wasn't a child any longer, and there was no way I was just going to sit there obediently while someone battered me. I began to struggle and lash out at Frankie, managing to get away from him just long enough to pull a nail file out of my bag. A second later, he was on me again and, when he grabbed hold of me, I tried to stab him.

Although I didn't really hurt him, I distracted him long enough to be able to run down the hall to the front door. But as I wrestled with the latch, Frankie caught up with me again, pushed me down on the floor behind the door and started smashing the door against my head. He was booting great lumps out of me, and jumping on me with the full weight of his body, and suddenly I felt a sharp, agonizing pain as he broke my nose.

A neighbour in the flat downstairs heard my screams and came running up the stairs. Semi-conscious and confused, I tried to call out when I heard her voice, but my face had been smashed to a pulp, and the only sound that came out of my cracked, swollen lips was a sort of croaking noise. I was still lying on the floor, wedged behind the door, and I could hear shouting as people tried to force it open. Eventually, they managed to reach in and pull me out, and they took me down to their flat and offered to call the police, which I refused – things with Frankie were bad enough without reporting him. When I eventually got home I was met at the front door by my daughter, who helped me into bed. I felt dreadful that she had to see me like that, and guilty because I was ruining her life with my inability to manage mine.

'I'll be fine,' I whispered, resting my head gratefully on the soft pillow. 'I just need to sleep. Go to bed.'

My daughter put a glass of water on the table beside me and went to bed, but she left me reluctantly – she was sure I needed to go to the hospital, but I just couldn't face the drama. Despite what I'd said, I wasn't really fine at all, and as soon as she'd gone, I eased myself painfully out of bed and swallowed all the pills I could find. I took five or six different types of pills, and I knew exactly what I was doing. I was absolutely weary and exhausted, and I just wanted to give up. I felt guilty about the terrible time I'd put my daughter through, having to sit and watch me gradually get beaten down by Frankie. I knew I'd thrown everything away. I wanted to come off the coke and try to get my life in order, but it was all just too hard. I'd tried and tried, but now I'd had enough. Surely no one could be expected to go on living a life like the one I was living, where every single day was a struggle and every time I dared think that something good was happening, it all turned to ashes in my hands?

I must have started slipping into a coma, because the next thing I remember was being carried downstairs. An ambulance must have arrived at some point, because I remember hearing a voice say, 'She's in a bad way. We need to get her to hospital quickly.'

The next thing I knew, I was lying in the A & E department of the local hospital having what I can only describe as an out-of-body experience. I was looking down on the scene from above, watching what was happening to my body as though it was someone else's, while the doctors and nurses tried to revive me. Frankie, my daughter and a friend of mine called Laura, were in a side room, and I seemed to be sitting in the corner watching them. Laura was beating Frankie on the chest and shouting, 'He's the fucking bastard that did this to her. Get him out of here.' I could see the anger and shock on her face, and the tears that were streaming down her cheeks. And I could see my daughter just looking at me and shaking her head sadly. Then I looked down at my own body, at all the cuts and bruises and at my broken nose, and thought, 'Thank God you're getting a rest at last.'

My thoughts were interrupted by the sound of Laura screaming at Frankie, 'Get out of the room!' and as he turned and walked away, I began to feel as though I was floating, and a sense of calm and warmth washed over me as I realized that I was taking my last breaths.

Then my attention was caught again by my daughter's face. She was sobbing and in a terrible state, and suddenly I remembered what it had been like to lose my own mum, how lonely and lost I'd felt, and I thought, 'I cannae do this to her. I cannae destroy my child.'

It was as though the thought dragged me back to reality, and at that moment I heard the doctor say, 'We've got a pulse.'

Chapter Fourteen

After I came out of hospital, Frankie moved away. But I still couldn't cope with my life, and I started taking ecstasy and speed as well as the cocaine and drink. I'd have dreadful hallucinations when I was coming down, and would hear and see things that made me think I was going off my head. Sometimes I'd hear Frankie's voice coming from somewhere in the flat, and I'd run from room to room in a panic, calling out to him and trying to find him. My friend Laura was staying with me, and she was wonderful. I was obviously suffering from paranoia, and she'd sit with me and say, 'Calm down. He's not here. It's all right, Liz. You're safe.' But I'd just stop for a moment, my eyes wide with crazy fear, and then whisper, 'He *is* here. Listen! You can hear him.'

Then, one day, Laura suddenly took hold of my arms, dragged me to a mirror and said, 'Look at the state of you, Liz. Just look at yourself! Go on, take a look in the mirror.'

She was right. I looked dreadful. But it was when she made me get on the scales, and I discovered that I weighed just six and a half stone, that she really gave me the shock I needed to make me finally understand what I was doing to myself – and to my daughter – and to make the decision to get myself cleaned up. I'd hit rock bottom, but the one positive legacy my father had given me was determination, and it was time for me to use it to pull myself up the other side and start living a more normal life.

It took me three months, and more than one suicide attempt, to get off the drugs completely, and they were among the most horrific three months of my life. But I was determined that I was going to succeed, and the only way to stop being a coke addict seemed to be to go 'cold turkey'.

My life became an emotional rollercoaster, and I'd lock myself away in my room and drink, and then phone my brother Alex and keep him up for hours in the middle of the night while I sobbed and told him what a mess my life was in. Poor Alex must have been exhausted, but he was fantastic. I don't think I would have got through that time if it hadn't been for his support.

Obviously, it was difficult enough trying to deal with the effects that stopping taking cocaine had on my body, but even more difficult was the fact that, without it, there was nothing to hold back the terrors of my past, which were threatening to engulf me. The memories would come flooding in, and would sometimes be so vivid that

I'd become convinced my father was there in the room with me. Night after night, I woke up soaked in sweat and curled up in a corner of my bedroom, in a blind panic and with my heart thumping.

After a while, I went to my doctor and asked if there was anything he could give me that would have the same effect on my mind as the cocaine did – blocking out the past and making it possible for me to deal with my life – without all the dangerous side effects. And he gave me sleeping tablets, which I've been taking ever since. Over the years, I've tried on a few occasions to do without them, but the night terrors always come back immediately, and they seem to be the lesser of the two evils.

Coming off the cocaine was difficult for another reason too. It meant that I had to find my identity, and discover who I really was when stripped of my drug-addict persona.

For three months, I travelled a dark, lonely and very scary road, but when I finally reached the end of it, I knew that it was a road I would never allow myself to travel down again.

Unfortunately, I didn't seem to be able to keep my finger off the self-destruct button for very long, and when Frankie turned up again one day, I opened the door wide and welcomed him in.

Right from the start, things weren't great between us. I knew that he was wrong for me, and that it was a mistake to let him back into my life, but somehow I couldn't help myself. I suppose I loved him, and I held on to the thought that he loved me, although I should have had the sense to realize that you don't treat someone you love the way he treated me. But, after all, what did I know about how people treat the people they love?

I'd been hooked on coke for three years and had just managed to stop taking it. Frankie told me that he had too, but I didn't believe him. Gradually, things got worse and worse, until I decided that I had to finish with him. One day, when he was in a particularly black mood because I couldn't get him any more money to buy coke, I waited until he left the house and then started to pack my bags. Even though he was staying at my place, I decided to leave temporarily – to give him some space and time to gather his things without all the shouting and screaming. I knew my daughter and I could stay with Laura for as long as necessary – in fact, her company was probably just what I needed at that moment.

A few hours later, as I was gathering together the last of my things, Frankie came home, and as soon as he saw the bags standing in the hallway, he started shouting and swearing at me.

'What the fuck's going on here?' he bellowed in my face.

'I'm leaving,' I answered, trying to keep my voice steady. 'I can't do this any more, Frankie. I'm going to stay with a friend. Take your time getting your stuff together and arranging somewhere else to stay.'

He took a swig of wine from the bottle he'd been carrying when he came through the door. 'Well, if you're leaving, I'm leaving,' he sneered, and picked up the phone to call someone to come and collect his stuff.

The mood turned increasingly sour and I decided that, given his anger and the fact that he'd been drinking, it was best for me to wait and let him leave first. But as he continued to drink he became more and more angry, and eventually started hurling things around the house and shouting abuse at me.

'Yous'll never get fuckin' anywhere,' he roared, his face so close to mine that the smell of the alcohol he was breathing over me transported me back to my childhood.

For a split-second, I was standing in front of my dad, with fear flooding like icy water through my veins as he worked himself into a fury before attacking me. But this time it wasn't my dad, it was Frankie, and I knew that my best chance of avoiding being hit was to say nothing. I stood there silently, not looking directly at him, praying that someone would arrive soon to collect his stuff and take him away, while he sat, still drinking from the bottle of wine and began flicking at his fingernails with a knife, which is when I started to feel really frightened.

I could almost see the big, black cloud that had settled

above Frankie's head, and I was taken by surprise when, after a while, he stood up abruptly and walked out of the front door without a word. As he started the engine of his car, my daughter was just returning from her friend's house, and he almost ran her over as he sped away, wheels spinning, down the road.

As soon as he'd gone, I knew that I had to grab my chance while I could, and I phoned the police.

'I want to report a drunk driver,' I told the police operator. 'He almost knocked my daughter down,' and I gave him the registration number of Frankie's car. Next, I phoned my friends and asked them to come and get my daughter and me as soon as they could, and then I began collecting together the last of our things. If the police arrested Frankie, it would buy us some time to get away. I knew I had to move fast, but a few minutes later, the front door opened and Frankie walked back into the hallway, almost hysterical with fury.

'I've come for my fucking stuff,' he shouted, before turning on my daughter and screaming at her, 'Where are my fucking car keys? What have you done with my keys, bitch?'

'Come on, Frankie,' I pleaded, trying not to show how frightened I really was. 'You've just been out in the car, so you must have had your car keys with you. She hasn't touched them.'

He didn't seem to hear what I was saying. He was completely out of control, shouting at my daughter and blaming her for everything that had happened. Then he stopped, as abruptly as he'd started, took his bag and left.

'Quick, grab whatever you can carry,' I told my daughter as soon as the door had slammed behind him. 'We need to get out of here. Now.'

I walked into the living room, leaving her closing a suit-case in the hallway, and at that moment the front door flew open again and Frankie came bursting back into the hall, screaming obscenities at us both. He was carrying a black can in one hand, and a few seconds later I could smell petrol.

Rushing out of the living room, I watched in horror as he started throwing the contents of the can everywhere – in the hall, the bedroom, the kitchen and the living room. I felt sick with fear. The smell of petrol filled my lungs so I couldn't breathe, and the fumes were stinging my eyes as I began grabbing armfuls of dirty washing from the wash basket in the bathroom and throwing them on to the floor in a desperate attempt to mop up the black pools of liquid that covered every surface. But there was just too much petrol everywhere. It was running in little rivers across tables and soaking into chairs and cushions, and I knew that I wasn't really getting rid of it, all I was doing was transferring some of it from one surface to another.

'I'll lock yous in,' Frankie was screaming, 'and then I'll torch the house with yous in it.'

My daughter was trying to get the can out of his hand, struggling with him and shouting at him to stop, but he just pushed her out of the way.

Choking, and almost blinded by the tears that were streaming down my face, I flung open a window and started throwing petrol-soaked towels on to the ground below, sobbing and shouting over my shoulder, 'Please, Frankie. Just think what you're doing. Stop it, please, Frankie.'

He paused for a moment, and I turned to look at him. The glare he gave me was filled with pure hatred, and all of a sudden he grabbed me from behind, pulled me away from the window and threw me into a corner of the hallway and started to throw petrol directly over me.

There was a fierce, burning pain in my chest when I tried to breathe in, and it felt as though my skin was already on fire. I began frantically to rip off my clothes, although I knew it was too late. He was going to lock my daughter and me in the flat and set us on fire. We weren't going to get out of there alive, and we weren't going to be the only ones. Images of all the other people who lived in the block of flats flashed in front of my eyes, and I felt a terrible sadness for them, but my main concern was to save my child.

'Frankie, please,' I begged him again, trying to hold my breath as I spoke and to stop the suffocating fumes seeping down into my lungs. 'Please let her go. None of this is her fault. Please, Frankie. You know that it's the last thing I'm ever going to ask you.'

He just laughed, and began pouring a trail of petrol along the hallway, out of the front door of the flat, down the stairs and out of the building. Like a flash, my daughter rushed down the stairs after him, slammed the outer door shut behind him and started to search around desperately for something to jam it closed. But she couldn't find anything, and as she ran back up the stairs towards me, she was shouting, and we both became aware that Frankie was pouring petrol all over the door.

Running back into the flat, I grabbed the telephone and called the police. As I was dialling the number, I could hear the outer door downstairs slamming open and, a moment later, Frankie was standing in the hallway of the flat holding a cigarette lighter.

'Please – Frankie!' I shouted, reaching out towards my daughter, who was standing in front of him in the hallway, ashen faced and too terrified to move.

'I told you,' he sneered at me. 'I'm going to torch this place.'

Suddenly, the front door burst open behind him and two men came flying through it.

'Right, everybody out,' one of them shouted, grabbing Frankie's arm and forcing it roughly up his back.

It was a few moments before I could understand what was happening, and then I pushed my daughter towards the front door and, sobbing with relief, watched her run out of the flat to safety.

Slowly it dawned on me that the men were policemen, and as one of them hustled Frankie out of the building, the other helped me rip off my remaining clothes, wrapped me in a coat and led me down the stairs to a police car.

It turned out that after I'd made the phone call about a drunk driver, they'd spotted Frankie's car as he was driving home from the garage up the road and followed him. But despite the terrible ordeal that Frankie put us through, and the fact that he risked the lives of everyone else in the flats, he didn't ever go to trial. It was something to do with legal technicalities and a file mix-up between stations. Whatever the reason, it simply reinforced the message I'd been receiving all my life – that people who did terrible things to me didn't need to be punished because I didn't really matter. My lack of importance had been ingrained in me throughout my life – by my father's treatment of me, and my mother's apparent indifference to it, and by what I consider to be the failure of the social services to rescue my siblings and me from what was clearly an extremely dysfunctional and unhappy home. Although, on one level, I know I'm as important as anyone else, I still sometimes find it hard to remember that fact, and to demand the respect I deserve. A feeling of worthlessness is a terrible legacy to give to any child because, whatever happens in that child's life, there will always be a part of their brain that believes that, in the greater scheme of things, they don't really matter.

The incident with Frankie did, however, give me a wake-up call. I knew that, if the police had arrived just a few seconds later, my daughter and I would certainly have been burnt to death. It felt as though I'd been given another chance to get my act together and start concentrating on looking after my child, and myself. So, after staying with friends for a while, I moved into a house for the homeless, and then into a council flat.

It was a grey, drizzly day when the man from the council offices took me to see the flat, and as I stood at the window looking out listlessly over the town, I felt a sudden sickening shock in the pit of my stomach, as though someone had punched me hard and knocked the wind out of me. Turning away from the window, feeling dazed, and fighting back tears, I said, in as normal a voice as I could manage, 'I don't want to live here. Have you got somewhere else?'

The man from the council continued to gaze out of the window for a while and then he shrugged and said, 'It's this or nothing.'

'Please,' I whispered, wiping away the tears that had begun to spill down my cheeks, and pointing in the direction of a nearby block of flats. 'Please, don't make me sign for this flat. My wee brother died just over there. I couldn't bear to live here and see the flat he died in every time I looked out of the window.'

He turned and looked at me for a moment and then shrugged again, saying, 'As I say, it's this or nothing.'

I knew that the alternative really was 'nothing', so I signed for the flat and moved in with my daughter, knowing that I was probably moving into the worst possible place to try to get my head together and make a fresh start.

To begin with, I was almost too frightened to breathe in case Frankie tracked us down. When we moved in to the new place, we had nothing, not even beds to sleep on, and we spent the first few nights on bare floorboards, lying on pillows and wrapped in quilts, hugging each other for warmth and comfort. Most of our belongings had been ruined by the petrol that had been poured all over them and they couldn't be saved. I seemed to have gone full circle, and it felt as though I was back in the same position I'd been in when my daughter was born, with nothing to give her except my love. The difference was, she wasn't a baby any more; she was fifteen years old, and love was no longer enough. She needed so much more than I could give her.

I was determined to get out of that flat and into a private let, and I started working two jobs to try to save enough money for a deposit. It wasn't long, though, before I realized that I couldn't work at that pace and take care of my daughter in the way she needed to be taken care of. At one point, I became so desperate and exhausted that I just couldn't cope any more, and I tried to kill myself again. However, as before, I failed, and one night not long afterwards, I sat holding my daughter, my face soaked with tears, and told her that I was sending her to live with Iain's mum for a while so that I could concentrate on saving for a place of our own. I'd bought her a mobile phone as soon as her dad and I had separated, so that he could contact her directly, without having to go through me. And although I've always felt guilty about separating her from her dad, in reality I know that it was up to them to make arrangements to see each other.

Iain's mum had always been good to me when Iain and I were together, and she adored her granddaughter and spoilt her rotten during the six months she looked after her.

Then, when I'd finally saved enough and was able to move out of the council flat, with its daily reminder of my brother's tragic death, and into the privately let flat I'd longed for, my daughter came home, and I began to think that we might just make it after all.

Chapter Fifteen

In time, I started to recover from everything that had happened over the previous year, but, as Christmas approached, I became more and more upset at the thought that I'd used every last penny of the money I'd saved as a deposit for the flat and didn't have any left over to buy a present for my daughter. I felt terrible, and the guilt just kept growing inside me like a fungus, until I was so lost in a black cloud of depression and self-hatred that I decided she'd be better off without me, and two days before Christmas, I slit my wrists. This was my most drastic attempt at suicide yet, but it reflected my mood, which had plunged lower than ever in the few months that had just passed. The shock of Shuggie's death and my own near-miss at the hands of Frankie had been hovering in the background for some time and, as ever, once I seemed to be on the road to recovery and should have been feeling settled, that was when it all engulfed me. I recognized the pattern now: it was almost as if the promise of better times ahead sent me into a meltdown – but I suppose that is the result of a lifetime of feeling unworthy.

Looking back on it now, this suicide attempt seems an extraordinary thing to have done, and it makes me hot with shame when I think of how deeply traumatized my daughter would have been – 'Merry Christmas. Your mother's dead' – and of how selfish and stupid I was being. But it was an action born of true despair and, once again, I have to thank the guardian angel that seems to be watching over me for making sure I didn't die.

Not long after that, my daughter started college, and I began a part-time psychology course in an attempt to understand what was going on in my own head. I was still working two jobs, and after a while I felt as though there was too much pressure on me and I gave the course up. I was at last beginning to be able to identify the triggers that set me off into a spiral and I knew that, when I took too much on, I became particularly vulnerable.

And then I met Scott. We've been together for six years now, and married for two, and I feel that I've found my soul mate. I didn't want a man in my life when I met Scott but, one day, after we'd gone out together a few times, I was starting to explain to him a bit about my life when he interrupted me.

'But I remember you,' he said. 'I remember you from when we were little. I used to hang about with your brother Alex, and my cousin's dad ran about with your dad. I remember coming to your door for Alex one day and your mum shouting, "Who the fuck's that?" and the next thing I knew, a vodka bottle came flying past my head and smashed on the ground behind me. So I know what your background is. You were a stunning-looking girl. I always thought you were dead pretty, and dead nice.'

It felt like coming home. We'd both been through horrible times and come out on the other side, and being able to talk openly to someone who knew the people involved and who didn't judge or criticize gave me an enormous sense of release. Our relationship developed from that moment, and it was only a couple of weeks later that he asked me to move in with him.

There have been occasions when I've locked myself away, but we can spend weeks, or even months, together 24/7 and not get sick of each other's company. We're such kindred spirits that, although we only got married two years ago, I feel as though I've been married to him from day one.

It was a huge step for me to put so much trust in one person, and it still scares me. However much Scott tries to reassure me, I'm so afraid he'll let me down, although, perhaps now, if he did, I'd have the strength to carry on. It feels as though the lost wee girl inside me is finally opening up and stumbling around in the big, wide world, and becoming a woman.

My mum was right when she told me just before she

died that, one day, I'd know someone called Scott. It's spooky to think that she might actually have been able to look into my future and see him. She was certainly right when she said I was going to have a hard time – so perhaps I'm on the verge of the wonderful life she could see for me too.

My life has left its scars on my body as well as on my mind. The years of my father's abuse resulted in broken bones that didn't heal properly and in internal damage that will affect my health for ever. I don't think I'll ever be completely free of the post-traumatic stress disorder and bouts of depression I suffer from, or from the effects of drug abuse, or the terrible migraines that occasionally make me have to shut myself in a dark room for three or four days at a time, or the blackouts I started having more recently.

One day, I was standing in the kitchen cooking, and the next thing I knew I was lying on the floor, without any memory of how I'd got there. It was really frightening, particularly when I realized that I could have been lifting a pan of boiling water when it happened. I decided I must have fainted for some reason, and didn't think much more about it.

Then, one morning not long afterwards, I jumped out of bed, and went into my daughter's room to wake her up for college. I was obviously too late and just as it was dawning on me that she must already be up and having breakfast downstairs, everything suddenly went black. All I can remember is sliding down the wall, until I was half-sitting and half-lying on the floor, the sweat lashing off me. After a few minutes, I managed to crawl into my daughter's bed, and I just lay there, shaking from head to toe, until I came to. Then, when I was conscious again, I started hyperventilating; my whole body was trembling uncontrollably, and I thought I was having a stroke. My fingers curled up into claws, my legs became stiff and rigid, and I couldn't draw any air into my lungs. Trying to fight back the panic, I crawled out of the bed and phoned the hospital's A & E department, and a doctor talked me through how to breathe until I could feel myself beginning to calm down.

It was really scary, and it still happens from time to time. I've hit the floor without any warning when I've been blow-drying my hair, and on one occasion I was drinking a cup of tea and had to shout for my daughter to take it out of my hands, as I felt myself starting to hyperventilate. Apparently, it's part of the post-traumatic stress disorder I suffer from because of what happened to me as a child. Now, I always keep my mobile tucked into my trousers, so that if I do fall, I can dial someone for help as soon as I come to, and I only ever have a shower when there's somebody in the house with me.

The worst of it is that I was working as a carer when the blackouts started and I had to give it up. It was a job I loved, but I realized I couldn't do it any more, because the blackouts happen suddenly, without any warning, and it was just too dangerous. But I'm desperate to get back to some kind of work again, not least because, if I don't keep busy, the demons start pushing open the doors in my mind and filling it with fear and anxiety until I can't sleep and can't even think straight.

I was working long hours as a carer, but leaving someone with a smile on their face was a reward in itself. Sometimes, though, the work proved to be just too stressful. For example, I was visiting one lovely girl who had mental-health problems, and I'd been warned that there might be something going on between her and her dad. I'd told the company I was working for that I wouldn't go out to the home of anyone who was an alcoholic, and I was shocked when they asked me to visit this girl, because they knew my background. But I went to her home anyway, and she told me that her dad was sleeping on the floor because he was homeless. I thought I was going to have a panic attack right there on the spot, and I knew I had to get out of there right away. I felt really angry that she was being shown a lack of care similar to that which I felt had ruined my life when I was a child. That poor girl couldn't even cook or look after herself, and she should have been in some sort of sheltered housing, not living alone with only unskilled people like me being sent out to help her. How could they just leave her there like that, knowing that her dad might be interfering with her and that she wasn't capable of defending herself?

I realize now that I got hooked on cocaine because it helped take the pain away when nothing else would, although, of course, in reality it only created a worse problem than the one I was trying to solve. I used to be able to block out some of my waking nightmares by working every day until I was too exhausted to think, but when I was too ill to work, there was nothing to hold the floodgates closed any more, and all the horrific memories and thoughts came pouring into my mind. It was just as though a dam had broken, releasing a surge of swirling black water that was going to drown me. The cocaine helped to keep the floodgates almost closed, although the price I paid for that was to be pushed down a path of self-destruction that would probably have killed me if I hadn't suddenly been able to see my life for what it had become and make the decision to stop.

I've talked to psychologists, although I've always found it difficult to go into details about my father's abuse, but, since I came off the cocaine, my doctor's been brilliant. He's held my hand throughout it all, and I've got a lot to be grateful to him for. However, there are still nights when I can't get to sleep, even though I've taken my pills. And every single night, whether I've taken them or not, I'm afraid to go to sleep, because when the nightmares come, my dad's in the room again. I did try to come off the pills at around the time I met Scott, but when I woke up from a nightmare one night and saw Scott lying in the bed beside me, I thought it was my dad, and I started lashing out and punching him, and then jumped out of bed and cowered in a corner like a terrified child.

If I don't sleep, I can't deal with the day, and then I just lock myself in my room and cry. It isn't that I get depressed for no reason, or because my life's shite; I'm depressed because of all the things that have happened to me. I don't want to take anti-depressants, because I don't want to become a vegetable. I can rationalize my sadness and understand it, and I know I've got to deal with it and keep my head above the water, although sometimes just doing that is completely exhausting.

One doctor I saw taught me self-hypnosis, which helped a bit. During my first appointment with him, though, I felt myself starting to panic, just sitting in his room. I didn't know what was wrong with me at the time, and it was only later that it dawned on me that the walls were painted the same colour white as the walls my dad used to bounce me off when he thrashed me in the hallway at home.

Simply being reminded of that made me feel as though I was about to get one of his slaps.

Then, when the doctor actually hypnotized me, it was his turn to get a fright. He was trying to reach a certain part of my memories and, suddenly, I was facing a line of closed doors. In my mind, I was running from one door to another, hitting them and trying to find a way out, and I started to hyperventilate. The doctor brought me straight back out of the hypnosis, and explained that we'd been trying to go into a part of my mind that's closed, and that opening those doors might prove dangerous for me. Some of them are gradually creaking open a wee bit now, but most of them are probably best left shut, with whatever horrific memories lie behind them kept locked safely away.

In fact, one key that unlocked some more doors a few years ago was asking to see my social work files. All the files are kept in the social work department's archives, and I had to wait months before I got a letter giving me an appointment to go and collect them.

As the day approached, I found it increasingly difficult to sleep. I knew that my memories of my childhood were real, but somehow it felt as though what was written in those files would validate them. And perhaps I was hoping to read something that would explain why no adult had

ever come to my rescue and plucked me out of the nightmare I had lived through for all those years.

At long last, the day arrived and I sat waiting in a room
that smelled of stale neglect, looking round at the book-
lined walls and piles of files that almost covered the floor,
feeling sick and trying to stop my legs shaking, until I was
called up to the desk. The man on the other side of the
table looked at me over the top of his spectacles and
handed me a file, sighing and shrugging his shoulders in
a slight gesture of helpless regret as he said, 'What can I
say?' I didn't know what he meant, so I couldn't think of
anything to say in response. I took the file he was holding
out to me, went back to my seat and started to read.

Immediately, my heart began to race and I felt tears
welling up in my eyes. I couldn't cry there; I couldn't let
anyone see how hurt and abandoned I was feeling. So I
bit my lip and carried on reading until, a few minutes
later, I stopped again, barely able to breathe. The details
of my horrific childhood were staring me in the face, the
story told in words that were blurred by my unshed tears
as I tried to focus on the pages.

I gave a small, apologetic cough to attract the man's
attention, and then, fighting to keep my voice steady, said,
'Excuse me. I'm sorry but . . . I can't read these here.
There's too much to take in. Can I take them home?'

I knew that I simply couldn't sit there and read through

the entire file with a total stranger sitting facing me across the table, however sympathetic his expression. All the terrible memories were coming flooding back, and I felt as though I was going to pass out.

'Well . . . yes, I suppose so,' he said, hesitantly, and then looked at me with a sad, kind smile before adding, 'You know, if you need anyone to talk to, you can give me a call.'

I knew he was trying to help, but I suddenly felt as though I had to get out of there fast, before I had a full-blown panic attack and broke down completely. So I just nodded, and then gathered up the papers, clutched the file to my chest and walked quickly towards the door and out of the building before he had time to change his mind about letting me take them away with me.

As soon as I got home, I sank on to a chair and started to read, my disbelief growing as I turned each page. It seemed to me that there were so many clear signals that all was not well in the family. I sat there feeling strangely detached, as though I was reading about some other little girl, and my heart was breaking at the thought that she could have been saved from all the terror and suffering of her childhood if only someone had acted on her behalf.

Reading what the social workers had written, it felt as though the child I used to be was being coldly dissected, and her situation picked over without any real understanding.

A cold anger began to creep over me at the thought that a vulnerable and fiercely unhappy child was left at the mercy of that monster of a man, even after he'd been convicted and sent to prison for 'lewd and libidinous behaviour' – the abuse of his own daughter.

I had asked for help, but my father had still managed to manipulate me and make me feel that leaving my mother to cope alone was selfish. So I'd gone home, which meant having to put up with more abuse and violent attacks after my dad was released from prison. I know that going back home had been partly my decision, because I wanted to protect my mum and my young brothers – but I was just twelve years old. Someone should have done something that would have spared us from the appalling abuse and misery that haunted every single day of our lives for the next few years, and from the deep scars that I still have to this day, and will probably continue to have for the rest of my life.

As an adult, I struggled day after day to find reasons to keep going, and there were five occasions when suicide appeared to offer the only way out from the hamster wheel I seemed to be trapped on. Then, in 2005, my daughter gave birth to a son, and a year later to a daughter, and the births of my grandchildren finally made me realize that suicide is never again going to be an option for me. My daughter and grandchildren mean more to me than anything else in the world, and I know that I have to stay strong for them. I've seen how evil life can be, and it's my job to watch over the people I love and keep them safe, and to make sure that my grandchildren have the best future they can possibly have. I'm still fighting, and I don't ever plan to give up.

After I read my social work file, I talked to a lawyer and then started an action against the social work department for failing to protect me from my father when I was a child. They didn't answer the letters sent to them by my lawyer, and just kept putting off dealing with any of it until, eventually, they produced some documents with great chunks of notes missing and lines blacked out, which they claimed related to other members of my family, although they'd left in lots of other details about them.

I had to have an assessment by a psychiatrist for a psychiatric report in support of my claim. I couldn't sleep for several nights before my appointment, because I was terrified that I was going to be told I had schizophrenia, like Shuggie. The psychiatrist wrote in her report that I'd been subjected to one of the worst cases of abuse she'd ever come across, but it was a huge relief when she assured me that I wasn't suffering from schizophrenia. And, with that major worry out of the way, it didn't seem quite so bad to be told that I had severe depression and post-traumatic stress disorder.

Next, an independent social care consultant reviewed all the available information from the social services' files, and stated that it was his opinion that there *were* grounds for a claim of negligence against the social services. Everything seemed set to go to court. The pressure of it all was enormous, and I longed for it to be over, but I was driven on by the thought that some sort of justice was finally within my reach. It had taken the social work department more than two years to produce the files we'd been asking for – and, even then, they were incomplete – but finally it looked as though someone was going to be held accountable for what had happened to me.

Before the lawyer took my case to court, he sought advice from an advocate and, out of the blue, the news came back that my claim would be time-barred. Apparently, a court action like mine has to be raised within three years of the act of negligence occurring, or, if the victim was a child, within three years of his or her sixteenth birthday.

I was stunned. How could things have dragged on for so long and got so far without anyone raising the issue of this law, which, as far as I can gather, has been done away with everywhere except Scotland? But that was that; it was the end of the line as far as I was concerned. Apparently, the courts will sometimes allow a late claim on the grounds that the person didn't previously know that they had a case to make. But because I'd consulted a lawyer some years earlier about the possibility of claiming compensation for the criminal injuries inflicted on me by my father, it was considered that I *should* have known then that I could sue the local council – the fact that no one even mentioned it at the time was apparently immaterial.

In fact, my criminal-injuries claim dragged on for years, too, and has only very recently been resolved. The initial case failed on the grounds that no payouts are made for criminal injuries that occurred before 1979 if the victim lived under the same roof as his or her abuser. So, according to the law, if you were a child who was abused before 1979, by a neighbour, for example, you'd be entitled to claim compensation for criminal injuries, but if the abuse took place day after relentless day at the hands of your father in your own home, that's just too bad. I don't know what the reason is for that particular cut-off point, or if it's just a randomly selected date, but it didn't seem to be relevant to my case anyway because, after my father came out of prison in 1977, he continued to abuse me for more than four years, until I was sixteen years old. And it was the fact of his continued abuse after 1979 that formed the basis of my appeal against the Criminal Injuries Compensation Authority's decision.

When the appeal hearing finally took place, it was as

gruelling and distressing as I'd known it would be. My brother Alex was there as a witness and to support me, and I thought my heart would snap in two when he broke down in tears as he talked about some of the effects Dad's behaviour had had on him, and how, as a young man, he had been unable to develop any real sense of personal identity because of what he'd been through.

But when I heard the board's decision, a shiver ran down my spine, and it felt as though someone had wrapped their arms around me and said, 'We believe you, and we're sorry.' Finally, someone had listened to what we were saying, and Alex and I stood in the corridor outside and hugged each other, tears streaming down our faces.

The financial compensation I was awarded wasn't a large sum of money, but it felt as though I'd won the lottery, because the emotional reward of winning my case was enormous.

However, as far as my case against the social services was concerned, I hit a brick wall – 'It's time-barred. Sorry. Go away.' In fact, it's actually been what's called 'cysted', which apparently means that, if the law *does* ever change – and assuming that I'm still struggling on if/when that happens, and that I haven't given up or died – I can try again.

Every knockback from the legal system, every time I'm told, 'I sympathize with your case. I'm sorry for what you've been through, but there has to be some cut-off point for paying compensation, and unfortunately you've just missed it,' it makes me feel as though nobody's really listening to me. All I want is for someone to say, 'We're sorry. We let you down when you were a vulnerable, frightened and desperately unhappy little girl. You asked for our help and we didn't do the right thing.' I just want someone to acknowledge what I had to live through all those years.

Quite apart from the sexual abuse, there was the terror I felt every time my dad thrashed Alex or Shuggie and I thought, 'Is it today? Is this the day he's going to kill one of them?' I lived constantly under the crushing weight of responsibility for their safety. I thought it was my job to look after them and to help them grow up to be good people, and I had an overwhelming sense of guilt because I didn't know how to stop them being hurt.

When you're living through a nightmare like the one I lived through, you don't really talk about what's going on. You just keep your head down and try to deal with each new horror as it arises. So it wasn't until years later, when we were adults, that we could finally talk to each other and share the burden a bit. Being the youngest, Alex, Shuggie and I were left behind in the house together a lot of the time and, as the oldest of the three, I knew that it was my job to protect them. However, I'd always felt I hadn't done enough, and that I'd let them down.

I don't think anyone ever really comes to terms with having been abused as a child. If you're lucky, you learn to live with it. But it stays with you for ever, in one way or another, and it colours every aspect of your life. Abused children grow up thinking that they don't matter, that they're simply there to be used by other people in whatever way they want to use them. It doesn't help to be told that you can't take your grievances to court; it's like saying that no one is going to accept responsibility for what happened to you. And, once again, that reinforces the message that *you don't really matter*.

When people hear about children having been abused, they're shocked and upset, but I don't think it's possible to imagine what it's actually like unless you've experienced it yourself. Every time I hear a report on the news or read something in the newspaper, the picture in my mind is quite clear, and I know exactly what that poor wee wretch has gone through. I'm constantly being thrown into a state of depression, knowing that children are still suffering at the hands of adults, and often at the hands of their own parents, the people who should be most dedicated to protecting them.

It used to be taboo to talk about sexual abuse, and about what happened behind the closed doors of people's homes. But gradually people are starting to realize that a lot of children have had the same sort of experiences I had when

I was a child, and that they carry the scars throughout their entire lives.

It was the job of social services to protect my brothers and sisters and me when we were children, and the signs that something was seriously wrong were clearly there for anyone to see. For whatever reason, I believe they didn't do that job properly, and I will never, ever, forgive them for that. I fear for all the other children who might be being failed by the social services, and by their communities and by neighbours looking the other way – and I feel as though I'm failing them too.

That's partly why I wanted to make a claim against the social services. I know everyone says, 'It isn't about the money,' but although the money would certainly be useful, because I do struggle financially, it's about so much more than that. It's about someone acknowledging that we have been let down. As a child, I was beaten, sexually abused and neglected, and was clearly terrified of my father and in desperate need of help. Maybe no one knew what to do. Maybe the people in authority at that time didn't have any experience or understanding of the sort of brutality we were living with. Maybe they just couldn't get their minds round the sheer, uninterrupted misery and evil that were handed out in my house every single day. I know that there are *still* children who are suffering like I did, and who are living through the same sort of nightmare that I lived through, and it breaks my heart. I feel as though there's a huge weight of responsibility on my shoulders, because if I don't keep plugging away for recognition and acknowledgement of the possible failures that left me and my young brothers in the power of a terrible, evil man, even after he'd served a term in prison, then who *is* going to help all the other victims of all the other evil men?

When I was twelve and told social workers that my dad was abusing me, it resulted in both my sisters escaping from the household, while I was left at home. It felt like no one seemed to think that what had been happening to me was any big deal, so I believed it was all somehow my fault and I should get on with it and stop complaining. I continued to live my young life in a constant state of fear and anxiety, on alert all the time in order to anticipate my dad's next move, deflect his anger away from my brothers, and protect my mum by making sure that I didn't do anything that would give Dad an excuse to take his rage out on her. The irony was that it didn't matter how hard I tried, because my dad didn't need an excuse. He was a very angry man, and I was never going to succeed in pleasing him.

I thank God that, unlike me, my daughter has a good man for a father. When I look back now, I regret some of things I threw away, and I feel guilty that my child lost her daily contact with her dad because of me. But I know that I have to forgive myself for that, because I was like a drowning person, panicking and lashing out and not realizing that I might be pushing away the one thing that could save me.

When I look at my daughter now, I see the woman I should have been. She's a really great girl, independent, confident and determined. I know that I've caused her pain that she should never have had to deal with, but, despite that, I can hold my head up high, because she's the living proof that at least there's one job that, overall, I did well.

I still have my faith in God, but I've lost my faith in humanity and my ability to trust. I've been let down so many times that I'm too scared to trust anyone. I know that I've got to get on with it, because I can't let my father win; I can't let him take up any more space in my mind and continue to control me.

There's still a lot of anger and hurt locked up inside me, and I've spent so many years stumbling around in the dark, trying to wrap my woman's body around the child inside me to protect her. But I know now that none of the things that happened to me as a child were my fault. I was too young to understand, and I'm not a bad person, so I don't have to blame myself. It's still a struggle, trying to live with the nightmares, and I'll probably always dread going to sleep at night, but I know that there's a lot of good in my heart and that killing myself would hurt too many people – and causing pain to other people would make me no better than my father.

Even to this day, if something nice happens to me, I'm immediately looking round to see where the next belt's coming from, because I just can't accept that something might simply be going right for me. I sometimes feel as though I'm going round and round in a revolving door, and every time I try to take a step out of it, someone kicks me back in again. The door isn't turning as fast as it used to though, and although it may never completely stop revolving, I won't give up hope that maybe, one day, I'll find my way out.

Chapter Sixteen

Last year, I went with Scott to visit the place my father lived for the last years of his life. Thinking about writing this book had opened the doors to so many memories, but there were still huge gaps in what I could remember, and many unanswered questions. I don't really know what made me feel that I needed to go there, and I made a few false starts, discovering at the last moment that I couldn't face the journey. But finally we were there, and my heart was in my mouth as I opened the heavy oak door of the church and stepped into the cool, dim light inside.

The only time I'd been to the village before was for my father's funeral, so it had few ghosts for me. But I can never think about my dad without feeling some sort of emotion, and later that morning I cried as I stood looking down at his grave – not tears of sorrow because he was dead, but tears of pity for the unhappy child I used to be.

In the years since my father's death, after I sat by his bedside at the hospital and told him I forgave him for what he'd done to me, I'd often wondered if I could ever really forgive him in my heart. Saying 'I forgive you' had cost me nothing; they were just words that I'd said for my own sake as much as for his. He'd cast a terrible black shadow over me throughout my entire life, and part of me had been afraid that if I didn't forgive him, he'd reach out from beyond the grave and blacken my soul with hatred.

I was sure that for someone to be able to sexually abuse his own child and beat and batter her so aggressively that he broke her bones as well as her spirit, and to destroy the lives of all his children before they'd even started, he had to have something wrong with him. Maybe there was a seam of evil running through his soul, or maybe he was mentally ill. Whatever the reason, I knew that the one thing I would never be able to come to terms with was the fact that he'd shown no remorse for what he'd done to us.

The priest at the church wasn't the one who'd offici-ated at my father's funeral, but we made some enquiries and discovered that a priest my father had known had subsequently changed his religion and was now retired. Later that afternoon, I was sitting in the car with Scott, outside the old priest's house, wondering if I dare go and knock on the door, when an elderly man came slowly along the pavement. He was leaning heavily on his stick as he walked through the garden gate, up the pathway and into the house.

Scott and I waited a few moments and, then, before I had time to change my mind, I opened the car door, stepped out on to the road, walked quickly up to the house and rang the bell. A few seconds later, I heard footsteps, and then the door opened to reveal a woman, wiping her free hand on her apron.

'Can I help you?' she said, her voice sounding brisk but not unfriendly.

'I . . . I wondered if I could talk to the priest,' I answered, swallowing hard.

'I'm afraid he's just about to have his dinner', the woman said. 'And he's rather tired. Perhaps you could call another day when . . . '

'I'm sorry', I interrupted her. 'I don't want to intrude, but I've come such a long way to see him. I'd be so grateful for just a few minutes of his time. Perhaps you could tell him who I am?' And I gave my maiden name.

The woman was clearly irritated, and with a terse, 'Wait here a moment,' she turned and stepped back into the house, closing the front door behind her.

I felt like the proverbial condemned man waiting to hear his sentence as I stood shivering on the doorstep. I knew that I'd never summon the courage to come back to this place again, and for some reason that I didn't understand, being able to talk to the priest that day seemed so important that even the thought of disturbing a tired old man who was about to eat his dinner wasn't enough to put me off.

A few moments later, the door opened again and the woman ushered us into the house.

'It's just for a few minutes,' she told me, as she led the way along the corridor and into a room, where the priest was sitting in an old leather armchair.

'I'm so sorry to disturb you like this,' I said as I bent down to shake the hand he was offering me. 'But I was so desperate to talk to you. Thank you for agreeing to see me.'

He shook Scott's hand and indicated for us to sit on the battered old couch that stood at right angles to his chair. Then, his eyes warm with sympathy, he turned to me and said, 'I was expecting you.'

He must have seen the look of surprise on my face, because he added hastily, 'Oh no, not today specifically. But some day. I knew you'd come looking for me some day. But I'm an old man now, and I hoped you wouldn't wait too long.'

He began to talk about my father, and it was as though he'd been holding a secret tightly inside him, waiting to be able to tell me so that he could let it go. It was obvious that it was a burden he'd been carrying reluctantly, and that he was relieved to be able to put it down at last.

The old priest had befriended my father in the months before his death, and Dad had obviously used the friend-ship as a sort of unofficial confessional, telling the priest everything he'd done to us as children. Although what he'd told him had been intended to be 'off the record', I believe that he hoped that one day I'd come searching for answers and perhaps finally find them.

'It was almost as though he was trying to shed himself of the weight of it,' the old man said. 'As though he knew that he was dying and wanted to release the dreadful secret that was locked inside him.'

The priest admitted that some of the unimaginably terrible things my father had told him had sometimes made him suspect that Dad was living in some dreadful fantasy land. Then, suddenly, he stopped talking, looked at me closely and smiled as he said, 'You're so like your father. I don't mean just in looks, although you do have the same piercing blue eyes that he had, but in your strength. It was as though your father just had to get his story out, because he was so truly sorry for what he did to you.'

He paused a moment, while I blew my nose and wiped the tears from my face, and then continued, 'I'm an old man now and I get tired very easily. But will you come back and talk to me again?'

I could see that he was exhausted, and so Scott and I got to our feet, thanked him and left, with promises to return. But I don't think I'll ever go back. Now I know that, before my father died, he *did* show remorse for what he'd done, everything has changed. And I can finally say, with my hand on my heart, 'I forgive you, Daddy.'

How to get help

The National Association for People Abused in Childhood

Set up to help provide support, training, information and resources to persons and organisations supporting people who have experienced ill treatment and/or neglect in childhood, this charity offers a range of services, from a free advice line, to guides to local and national support groups

Website
http://www.napac.org.uk/

Freephone
0800 085 3330

Acknowledgements

I want to thank Sandra, Lisa, Trevor, William, Abby, Kenneth and all the friends who held my hand through the tears and helped guide me through the dark times. I am grateful, too, to my daughter and grandchildren; to my husband, Scott, and to Nicole; to my uncle and aunt, who showed me what a real family is; and to the other members of my family – particularly my brother Alex and his wife – who have supported me and encouraged me to tell my story.

I would also like to thank my friend Thomas, who I know I will meet again one day; the politicians who have done their best to support me in my search for justice; my doctor, who has been a saint and a friend through it all; and John Mace, whose remarkable therapy – the Mace Method – recently helped me to get through some of my darkest hours.

And I am grateful to my dear friend Marcello and his wife Cathy, who gave up so much of their time to give me a voice; and to Jane Smith, who helped turn my whisper into a shout, as well as my publishers, particularly Carly

Cook and Josh Ireland, all of whom believed in me and helped transform my story into this book.

This book started with me trying to say goodbye to the world and ended as a healing journey instead. I have been fortunate to meet some wonderful people along the way, and I am grateful to those I have loved and lost, and to all those who have made me into the woman I am today.

More Non-fiction from Headline Review

DESTROYED

JAYNE STERNE

When eight-year-old Jayne left bomb-torn Northern
Ireland, her family stayed with relations and a distant
relative began a campaign of abuse so horrifying that
her world was shattered for ever.

And when the family moved again – her relative came
too. Raped repeatedly, beaten, abused and battered,
Jayne's life was a living hell.

One thing kept Jayne sane: the love and care of her older
brother, Stuart. But he had demons of his own, and Jayne
watched in despair as the boy who had always protected her
turned into an adult consumed by rage. Out of control,
Stuart went on to commit the 'Barbecue Murders',
one of the most terrible crimes of recent years . . .

Destroyed is the heart-stopping true tale of an innocence
stolen and a family torn apart – told by a woman who has
finally managed to confront her harrowing past.

Someone she knew
Someone she trusted
Someone who betrayed her

The devastating true story of a shattered childhood

NON-FICTION / MEMOIR 978 0 7553 1799 8

MUMMY, MAKE IT STOP

LOUISE FOX

Louise's childhood was a living nightmare.

Repeatedly sexually abused by her mother's out-of-control boyfriend, the little five-year-old was surrounded by evil.

Louise was beaten with belt buckles, starved and neglected as she suffered at the hands of both her mother and her mother's partner.

Finally, her tormentor was arrested. But her mother stood by him and Louise was dragged to visit him in prison, forced to sit on her abuser's knee and tell him how much she loved him and wanted him to come home.

The horror continued when her mother found a new partner worse than the last. Within months he was assaulting and eventually raping Louise.

Taken into care, Louise ended up addicted to drugs and selling her body. But the birth of her child saw Louise vow to turn her life around – and that is just what she did.

She broke free, and *Mummy, Make it Stop* is the true story of a brave spirit that refused to be crushed.

NON-FICTION / MEMOIR 978 0 7553 1850 6